How to Keep a Naturalist's Notebook

How to Keep a Naturalist's Notebook

SUSAN LEIGH TOMLINSON

STACKPOLE
BOOKS

Published by
STACKPOLE BOOKS
5067 Ritter Road
Mechanicsburg, PA 17055
www.stackpolebooks.com

Printed in China

Cover design by Wendy A. Reynolds

10 9 8 7 6 5 4 3 2 1

First edition

Library of Congress Cataloging-in-Publication Data
Tomlinson, Susan Leigh.
 How to keep a naturalist's notebook / Susan Leigh Tomlinson.—1st ed.
     p. cm.
 Includes bibliographical references.
 ISBN-13: 978-0-8117-3568-1
 ISBN-10: 0-8117-3568-0
 1. Nature study. 2. Drawing—Technique. 3. Animals—Identification.
4. Plants—Identification. I. Title.

QH51.T66 2009
508.072'3—dc22

                                                    2008034040

For Frances Tomlinson, Frances Williams, and Walt Schaller.
And for my students.

Note to the Reader

The identification and selection of any wild plant requires reasonable care and attention to details. Some plants may be toxic, and it is therefore safest to not gather any plants unless they have been positively identified by an expert. Because attempts to gather any wild plants depend on various factors controllable only by the reader, the publisher and author assume no responsibility whatsoever for adverse health effects of such failures as might be encountered in the individual case.

Contents

Preface

When I was in my twenties, I discovered nature. Well, what I really discovered first was a group of people who were avid amateur naturalists. I was living in a small west Texas town, looking for something to do on Saturdays, when, through circumstance, I was invited to go on one of their nature walks. They called themselves the "Midnats"—short for Midland Naturalists—and I found them delightful company. One of the leaders of the group was a kind, older, button of a woman named Frances Williams, and it so happened that she was one of the most respected birders in the state of Texas.

I knew nothing about birds or wildflowers or why the oldest trees in a town are almost always found in the cemetery,[1] but Frances and the others did. The depth of their collective knowledge, and Frances's especially so, was remarkable. And so, over the course of the next three years, I was an enthralled pupil on those weekly Saturday morning walks. I had grown up in New Mexico and west Texas and thought I knew something about my home ground—namely, that it was devoid of anything remotely interesting! But under the tutelage of the Midnats, I was astonished to discover that that subtle landscape was, in fact, brilliantly rich in nature.

I eventually moved away to attend graduate school, earning both a master's and a doctoral degree in geology. This in itself reflects an awakened interest in the natural world, since my previous, undergraduate degree was in studio art. I loved my new field of study, but I found that I really missed the weekly nature walks. There was no group of passionate local naturalists that I could find—no Frances—to take me on gentle, unhurried, guided tours of my new home ground in the Texas Panhandle Plains.

1. Frances explained that a cemetery often has some of the oldest trees in town—an important feature in west Texas—because it is one of the first places people plant trees when a town springs up, and one of the few areas resistant to development. I'm not sure whether she picked up this piece of knowledge from one of the many books and papers that she read, or whether it was her original idea, but it certainly seemed like a reasonable explanation to me.

A few years later, I became a college professor in charge of a brand-new interdisciplinary degree program in nature studies. As part of the curriculum, I created a course called Introductory Fieldcraft, designed to be very much like those Saturday morning walks—the focus being on thoughtful explorations into the field. I was a poor substitute for Frances and the Midnats, but I did my best to emulate their good example and teach the students how to identify plants and animals, record what they found, and put this knowledge about the natural world into a context that enriched their lives. At the center of the course curriculum was the field journal. And because of my combined science and art backgrounds, at the center of the field journal were drawings and detailed descriptions of the world they encountered.

I had a problem, though. A textbook did not exist for the sort of course I was teaching. There were books on drawing and keeping nature journals that were limited in content, but they seemed to be aimed primarily at a younger audience than my college students. There were field guides to birds and wildflowers, but while they offered information on the identifying characteristics of nature subjects, they did not actually teach much about the process of identification to the student just starting out. And there were books on how to use the journal as a literary springboard, but these did not offer anything on drawing and field identification. In short, what I needed was a book that combined all these things so that the student of nature would not have to buy several books, but one. So I set out to create my own.

Spring grackles

This book, *How to Keep a Naturalist's Notebook*, is the result. It is part lesson in the basics of sketching, part instruction in journal writing, and part walk through the process of identifying something and learning about it. It is not a manual on how to collect data for scientific study—most fields of science have specialized language and formats for recording data, and the serious students of science would do well to take courses in those disciplines. Nevertheless, this book offers instruction for keeping a detailed, exploratory notebook about the natural world. As a result, there is something in it for every kind of naturalist, from the backyard bird-watcher who wants to learn to sketch the visitors at his feeder to the seasoned field scientist who wants to learn to keep a nature journal with a literary and artistic bent. Although it is written primarily for beginners like my college students, I also wrote it mindful of a professional biologist I once knew who expressed frustration at her inability to draw birds in the field. This book is for both ends of that spectrum, and everyone in between, who might have an interest in learning to keep a comprehensive nature journal. It's the sort of book I wish I'd had after I'd moved to a new place and wanted to explore it, but didn't have a local group of naturalists to show me how to unlock the secrets.

Think of this book as a jumping-off place. It is designed to be an introduction to field drawing, identification, and journal writing—not the final word on any one of these. There are other, excellent books that go into more depth on each of these topics, and I've included some suggested reading in the bibliography at the end of this book.

I've included examples not only from some of my work, but also from that of some of my students as well. You'll see that you don't have to be a "professional" to create a lively, informative record of your experiences with the natural world. The students represented in this book were not art or science majors; there were a couple who were in the degree program in which I'm involved, Natural History and Humanities, but the rest were French, math, psychology, and engineering majors. The thread that brought them all together was a desire to learn something about the world in which they lived.

In addition to the illustrations, I've also tried to include enough explanation in the text for any readers who, like me, learn better when they understand the "why" behind the instruction. In any case, some of the chapters may be more useful to you than others. You may already possess some drawing skills, understand how to use a field guide, or know how to identify wildflowers. Take what you need from the book and use it to create a journal that suits you. But do get out there—the chances are good that your home environment is brilliantly rich in nature, too. Keeping a careful, thoughtful notebook about what you observe and learn may help you one day become a "Frances" of your own landscape.

Acknowledgments

I'd like to thank my students, who have always inspired me; they make teaching a joy. In particular, I'd like to express my appreciation to Delilah Clark, Jessica Meixner, Mary Porter, Robert Waller, Monica Warren, Jay Daniel, and Katy Watson, for generously providing me with their work for use in this book. I am indebted to John Sill, who was gracious enough to allow me to pass along his very useful instruction for bird proportions. Thank you, also, to Lisa Conturier, Nancy McIntyre, and Kurt Caswell, for reading early drafts of the manuscript. I'd also like to extend my gratitude to the Midland Naturalists for opening my eyes to the natural world. Most of all, I'd like to thank my husband, Walt Schaller, for putting up with my wildly diverse interests for all these years.

1. Getting Started

You don't need a lot of gear to get started on your journey into learning about nature. As Greg Brown points out in his song "Two Little Feet," John Muir went into the mountains with an old overcoat and a crust of bread, and he seemed to do all right. As much as I love gear, I have to remind myself sometimes that it isn't about having a lot of stuff; it is about the knowledge and experience I gain from observing and participating in the natural world. The tools required to start and maintain a naturalist's notebook are simple and few. At the most basic

> *We have no knowledge and so we have stuff and stuff with no knowledge is never enough to get you there.*
>
> —Greg Brown,
>   "Two Little Feet"

Davis Mtns   Spring 2005

end of the spectrum, all you really need is a writing instrument and some paper. Most of the time, in fact, all I carry is a sturdy notebook and a mechanical pencil.

That said, there are a few items you can add to your kit that will make your field experience easier and more enjoyable. I have used all of these, and continue to use most from time to time, depending on my needs. The list below is not a prescription but a suggestion based on my own experiences.

The Field Kit

FIELD NOTEBOOK

Over the years, I've tried out many different types of field notebooks, searching for the perfect blend of portability, ease of use, and paper "tooth"—the way the surface of the paper interacts with your writing or drawing instrument. What I have found is that in the realm of journals,[1] as in the rest of life, there is no such thing as a perfect solution.

A small, pocket journal works just fine if all I want to do is make short notes to myself about a piece of writing I'm working on at home or briefly describe a plant or bird I'd like to identify later. But I find small pages confining when I want to draw or write a longer piece. I just can't seem to be creative when I'm feeling spatially cramped by the page. This probably has more to do with the way my hand is supported when I draw, since I don't have a problem drawing *small*, just with drawing on a small page. So most of the time I carry a journal that is about 8.5 × 5.25 inches in size. Here again, however, I have different preferences and use a ruled journal when I plan to do more writing than drawing, and one with blank pages when I want to draw and paint.

For ruled pages, I prefer a notebook made by a company called Moleskine. There's no special reason for this—I just find that the line spacing and tooth of the pages suit me. Also, the pages are thin, so there are lots of them in a slender volume. Any ruled journal this size will do, however.

I also use, as my principal sketching/drawing/watercolor field notebook, the Moleskine Large Sketchbook. The pages have pretty good tooth, and they are stiff enough to hold up to light water coloring without buckling. However, it is a little pricey (simply because it has fewer pages than most similarly sized sketchbooks) and sometimes hard to find. I also prefer the Moleskine notebooks because they open flat. Spiral-bound notebooks will do this as well, and

---

1. I use *field notebook* and *journal* interchangeably, since virtually all of my "journaling" is done in the field.

many people enjoy using these. I'm left-handed, however, and find that the wire coil gets in the way of my hand, so I've never been able to work comfortably using such a notebook.

For an inexpensive, readily available field notebook to use for drawing and painting, the Strathmore 8.5 × 11.5–inch Hardbound Sketchbook is hard to beat. There are lots of pages because they are relatively thin, but they are stiff enough to handle a little water when I use my watercolor pencils (though they do buckle slightly). The tooth works very well with both pen and pencil and gives good results whether you are trying to draw a fine line or do a little shading. And since it is cheap, you don't feel like you are making a big investment when you buy one.

This last point is an important one. When you go into a book or art supply store, you'll often find rows and rows of fancy journals from which to choose. While I think what you ultimately pick will be a personal preference, I suggest you stay away from any that are too expensive. To journal well, you need to feel the freedom to mess up—often. Especially if you are learning to sketch or trying out writing ideas, many of your efforts will look half-finished and less than perfect. This is not only to be expected, it is a good sign, since it means you have the courage to try new things.

I've purchased my share of expensive journals with rich, textured papers on which to write. They are all still on my bookshelf, largely untouched. Every time I open one, I feel compelled to write something important in it—something befitting its esteemed status. The trouble is that the best journaling is often exploratory, sometimes random, and usually just plain routine. Fancy journals are not the place for the everyday, and the everyday world is a big part of what we are recording. In my notebooks, I have sketches of grasses, grocery lists, variations in sentences from poems that I am working on (over and over and over . . .). Not only are the expensive journals intimidating, it usually seems the snazzier the tome, the fewer the pages. And since you'll be carrying these notebooks into the field with you, where they are going to get kicked around quite a bit, tough and utilitarian is the better way to go. In the best of all possible worlds, you'll take your journal hiking, backpacking, fishing, canoeing, and so on, so you'll want one that can go the distance with you.

In summary, the features you want to look for in a notebook are as follows: inexpensive, durable, lightweight and not too big, good tooth, and plenty of pages. In the end, you'll develop your own preferences, of course, but if I had to pick only one journal, or one to start out with, I'd pick the Strathmore sketchbook. It is a good, inexpensive, all-around workhorse.

FIELD BAG

Like the journal, I've probably tried out every field bag on the market looking for the optimum fit between ease of use, portability (i.e. not too heavy), and amount of stuff it can hold. And, like the journal,

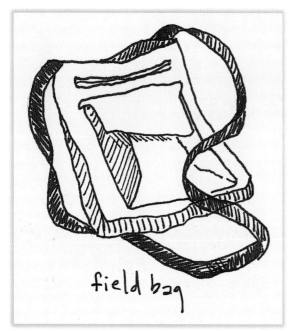

field bag

I've come to the conclusion that there is no such thing as the perfect bag. Instead, I have my specialized lumbar pack for trail running, my birding bag for trips devoted solely to that endeavor (I can stuff it with binoculars, field guide, and lunch), another lumbar pack for fly-fishing, a small see-through dry bag for canoeing, and my "everyday" bag.

My everyday bag is a bit of a misnomer, since I don't actually carry a bag every day. (I find it hard to convince myself to even carry a purse!) Whenever I do go for a walk in the local parks and trails with the intention of doing some sketching and journaling, however, it easily holds my field notebook, pencil box, eyeglasses, compass, and hand lens.

It doesn't matter what you use for your everyday bag (I go back and forth between a purse-sized shoulder bag and a small day-pack); it just needs to be one that is large enough to hold your notebook and some sketching supplies, but not so big that you feel a wave of panic at slipping it over your shoulder when you head out the door. There are a variety of possibilities on the market; just look for a bag that is durable and large enough to hold your notebook and a few extra items, and it should suffice. Whether you want a shoulder or a lumbar bag is your choice, but for what it's worth, for everyday use I've gravitated toward the shoulder system because it is easy to slip on and off.

DRAWING, PAINTING, AND WRITING TOOLS

You don't need anything especially fancy to make notes and sketches in your journal. Most of my sketching, in fact, is done with a mechanical pencil with a good eraser on top and filled with 0.5 mm HB lead. I find this sufficient for most of my needs. Even so, there are a few simple things you can put in your kit that could prove useful or enjoyable. Here is a short list of suggestions:

Ink Pens

Though artists once used nibbed pens and India ink for many of their field drawings, materials have become a lot more convenient. Although any inexpensive, waterproof, fine-lined, felt-tipped pens could probably suffice in a pinch, I find that they tend to skip a great deal and can be frustrating. The best pens for sketching are those made specifically for artists and drafters, which can be found in most artists' supply stores. I currently use one by Faber-Castell that comes in a variety of line sizes, but there are other companies that make equally good ones. My main criteria in choosing a pen, aside from the quality of line I can lay down on the paper, is that the ink is waterproof—that way I don't have to be concerned about my work running if the paper gets wet.

Pencils

As I said above, I do most of my sketching with a mechanical pencil. However, I sometimes also carry along some old-fashioned drawing pencils for any sketches that require shading techniques. They come in different hardnesses, with H being harder (lighter) and B softer (darker). I usually keep an HB, B, and 2B in my pencil box and find that these three suit all my shading needs.

Tools for Shading

For help in shading, I sometimes use something called a blending stump. These are pencil-shaped rolls of paper with pointed ends that do just what their name suggests. They can be found at any art supply store. I prefer a number 3 size for portability. You could use your finger in a pinch, but it doesn't work as well, and you'll probably leave smudges on the rest of the paper after you do your blending.

Erasers

For erasing—which you might need to do, either because you've made a mistake or for highlighting techniques—a soft white eraser works better than most. You only need a little bit, though, so I cut mine in half with a knife to save some space in my kit. Some people prefer a kneadable eraser because it makes it easy to control the area you erase. Try one out—you might find you prefer it, too.

Sharpeners

You'll also need a small pencil sharpener. I carry one that catches the pencil shavings rather than one that will dump them on the ground, since I want to be sure to leave the site clean for others to enjoy. Buy a small, good quality one. You would be surprised at how quickly cheap sharpeners quit doing their job.

Watercolor Pencils

It is sometimes nice to add a little color to field sketches, either in the form of colored pencils or watercolors. Fortunately, you can do both with one tool, the watercolor pencil. Use them like a pencil, add a smidgen of water, and *presto!* For ease of use in making every-day field notes, these are superior to lugging along boxes of watercolors to the field. It is not too much of an exaggeration to say that they have changed my life. (Of course, at some point you may decide that you want to use some real water-colors to make a real paint-ing, but that's a different book.)

My favorite watercolor pencils are made by Prisma-color. I've tried others, but these really do seem to work better than the others as *both* pencils and watercolors. Prismacolor sells a small starter set of a dozen or so that suits our purposes. Later on, you may want to pur-chase additional colors to supplement the basic set. As a side note, Prismacolor does not include purple in the starter set, and many students find this lacking, given that so many wildflowers are purple.

cackling &
canada geese

Fortunately, most art supply stores also sell the pencils separately, so it is a small thing to purchase a purple one to add to the set.

Brushes

To turn the pencils into watercolors, you also need a small brush. Here you want to spend a few dollars and buy a good one. It isn't necessary to have the best of the best, but you want one that will keep a good point after much repeated use. Go to a good arts and crafts store and look for a medium-priced brush in the watercolor brush section and you should be fine. I'd start with a number 2 round, but sooner or later you may find you want to add other sizes and shapes to your field kit arsenal.

I also have a favorite, big, fat Japanese watercolor brush that I use. Originally, I used it for painting in sky and cloud washes when I did watercolor landscapes. Now, however, I keep it around to brush away eraser residue—if I use my hand, it tends to smudge the drawing. A nice, fat brush sweeps the page and leaves it clean.

Pencil Case or Box

You might want a pencil box to keep all these tools together in your field bag. It isn't necessary to get something fancy, and it only needs to be big enough to keep it all together—too large and it becomes a burden to lug around. These are also generally available at any art supply store. Over the years I have gravitated to carrying one made by ArtBin that is roughly $10 \times 6 \times 3$ inches, but you may find this over-large at first. For a beginning kit that I put together for my students every year, I include a much smaller one that is only $8 \times 3 \times 2$ inches in size.

Compass

As I mentioned, I usually have a compass stashed in my field kit, not necessarily because I get lost easily, but because it is convenient to stick it in there and forget about it. If you want to learn mapmaking and orienteering, you'll need an orienteering compass. You can find one that is relatively inexpensive, but it needs a rotating base plate designed for orienteering, and you must be able to set its magnetic declination. If you go to a reputable outdoor shop and ask for an orienteering compass, they should be able to help you. Don't let the store clerk tell you that you need one that costs more than about $20, unless you really want the bells-and-whistles model. Two good compasses in the $10 to $20 price range are the Silva Ranger and the Brunton Classic. Either will be fine for a simple, throw-in-the-bag compass.

Hand lens (optional)

I also carry a hand lens around in my field kit. Aside from my failing middle-aged eyesight, there are plenty of good reasons for doing so. There is a whole world we can't see without this aid, and I like to take it out to look at insects, seed heads, feathers, and other curiosities.

When I was a practicing geologist, a hand lens was indispensable for identifying rocks and microfossils. As a result, the ones I use are professional models (10x and 20x Hastings triplets) and are a bit of overkill for everyday use. You can get a perfectly good one for around $15 if you want to add another dimension to your world. A 10x power doublet[2] is good for all-around use.

Another, less expensive, alternative is a pocket magnifier. A pocket magnifier consists of circular magnifying lenses that fold up into a small case much like the hand lenses. They start at 5x power, but go up to 10x and 15x power by stacking lenses. While the quality is not as good as professional hand lenses, it is probably sufficient for taking a closer look at grasses or flowers. At one-third the cost of a hand lens, this would probably be my pick for a first magnifier. You can upgrade later if you decide that you want better quality. Whether it's a hand lens or a pocket magnifier, I like to tie a piece of bright yarn or shoelace to it. That way if I drop it somewhere or accidentally leave it somewhere, I can spot it quickly when I look for it. (A shoelace is also a handy way to hang the magnifier around your neck.) Sources for hand lenses and pocket magnifiers can be found easily on the Internet.

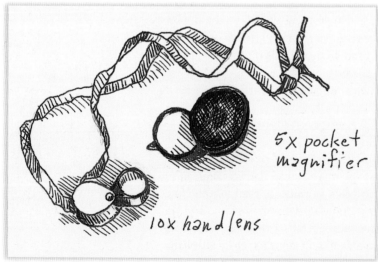

5x pocket magnifier

10x hand lens

2. "Triplet" and "doublet" refer to the number of lenses used in the magnifier.

Binoculars

A good pair of binoculars can go a long way toward helping you study the natural world, especially where birds and other animals are concerned. Unfortunately, good binoculars are expensive. Though others might disagree, I think cheap binoculars are usually better than none at all, so buy or borrow a pair and take them out to the field with you.

If you think you might be serious about your ventures into the field and you are in a position in your life where you can afford it, you should consider buying at least a good pair of entry-level bins.[3] While I will share a few things that will be useful to know when you go to buy them, I won't make any recommendations for specific brands. Binocular technology, like everything else, is continually changing and improving, and this year's top performer/best buy might not be next year's. Also, like most things, one person's needs might not be another's. Fortunately, there is a wealth of information available from a number of sources, so with a little research, you should be able to find a pair that suits your needs. (One good place to start is the Web site for the Cornell Laboratory of Ornithology, which not only has some very good information about binoculars in general, but also has reviews about specific brands and models.) In the meantime, here is a little information to get you started.

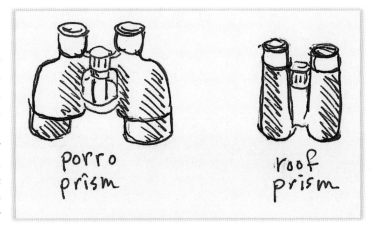

Porro Prisms and Roof Prisms

First, there are two basic designs: roof prisms and porro prisms. Roof prisms are shaped like an H, and porros are more like an M (see the above illustration for what I mean). Roof prisms are generally more compact and easier to make waterproof than porro prisms. Good roof prisms are also more expensive to manufacture than porro prisms of comparable quality. Consequently, for good, entry-level binoculars, you'll usually get a better value with porro prisms. Having said that, the very *best* roof prism binoculars are simply astonishing in their clarity—and carry an equally astonishing price tag.

3. "Bins" is birder slang for binoculars.

Magnification and Light Gathering

Binoculars have two sets of lenses: the oculars (the ones closest to your eyes and the parts of the binoculars that magnify) and the objectives (the ones farthest from your eyes). I'll talk more about the magnification in a moment, but for now I want to focus on the objective lens, which is, to many people's minds, the more important. The function of the objective is to gather light; the more light you can gather at dawn and twilight—the times when birds and other animals are most active—the better. The bigger the objective lens, the more light you will gather and the better you will see detail.

The rub comes when you pair the objective lens with the magnification of the ocular lens. The higher the magnification, the less light the binocular can transmit to your eyes. The amount of light that is transmitted is referred to as the exit pupil. There is a simple formula that describes this: the diameter of the objective lens divided by the magnification equals the exit pupil. For example, a 7×42 pair of binoculars (where the 7 refers to the magnification and the 42 refers to the diameter of the objective lens) has a light gathering potential of 6 mm. A bigger exit pupil means more light; therefore, a bigger objective lens or a smaller magnification will increase light, whereas a smaller objective lens or a larger magnification will have the effect of decreasing the amount of available light.

Many people make the mistake of assuming that higher magnification is always better. This is not the case, however, unless you want to sacrifice the overall quality of the image in low light. Furthermore, binoculars can be hard to hold steady at the higher end of magnification. And finally, the higher the magnification, the heavier the bins, which is an important factor to consider when you are lugging them around all day.

A good all-around magnification versus objective lens combination is the standard 7×42 pair of binoculars. For those who do a lot of hawk or pelagic (sea) bird observing, another popular all-purpose compromise is the 10×40. For those of us who want to own only one pair, 8×42 makes a good compromise.

Field of View

Field of view refers to how much of the "field" is in your "view" at a distance of one thousand yards. In its simplest and most practical sense, it is the area you see when you look in the binoculars. In bins with a wide field of view, for example, you will see a larger area of a tree you are viewing than you will looking at the same spot with bins that have a narrower field of view (say, five feet in the first case as opposed to three in the second). A wide field of view is helpful for locating elusive birds, either in those pesky trees or in the wide blue sky. Generally speaking, the higher the magnification and the smaller the objective, the narrower the field of view. People who spend a lot of time in dark woods looking for tiny warblers often like bins with a wide field of view; after all, if you're fairly close to the bird, you don't need that much magnification.

Truthfully, though, I've never been particularly concerned about field of view. I take a more Zen approach to my warbler-watching: either I'm going to find it when I raise my bins to look, or I'm not. And yes, I'm sure I've missed a few this way, but far fewer than you'd think. (We'll discuss binocular technique in another section, Preparing the Kit.)

Eye Relief

Eye relief is the distance from the surface of the ocular to the focal point inside the binocular. This is pretty meaningless to most of us, so suffice it to say that if you wear eyeglasses or sunglasses, without long eye relief, the field of view you actually see in the bins will be tiny. This is simply because with glasses your eyes are farther back from the point at which everything comes into focus. Eye relief can range from as little as 5 mm (poor) to as much as 23 mm (very nice, but probably over the top in what you need). A general rule I use is that the larger the surface area of the ocular, the longer the eye relief. Most eyeglass wearers will want binoculars that have a minimum of 14 mm of eye relief. Something in the range of 17–19 mm is even better. Almost all good entry-level to high-end binoculars have pretty good long eye relief these days, but it is still a good thing to look for in the specifications when you buy. Even if you don't wear glasses now, you might someday (or you might enjoy wearing sunglasses in the field, as I do), and good binoculars can be a long-term investment.

Interpupillary Distance

Interpupillary distance is the minimum distance between the oculars when the binoculars are folded in. Most people will never give this a second thought, but if you are like me—somewhat beady-eyed—this distance can be the difference between a pleasant day in the field and frustration. If the interpupillary distance of your bins is too wide for your eyes, no matter how hard you try, you aren't going to get those two circles to become one field, a problem that will leave you dizzy and dissatisfied. It is always good to try out gear when you get a chance; however, if you don't have this opportunity and you plan to order your bins, you might want to try measuring your own inter-pupillary distance (the distance between the center of your pupils) to make sure you get something you can actually use. Again, though, *most* good entry-level and high-end bins don't seem to be a problem for me, so I suspect they'll be okay for most of you, too.

Optical Quality

The most important criterion for selecting binoculars is the quality of the lenses themselves. It is, in the final analysis, what you end up paying for in a good pair of bins. A well-made lens will have extra-low dispersion (ED) and high-density (HD) glass to provide clarity and contrast as well as "true" color, and will also have special antire-flective coating(s) to ensure more light transmission. When you look through binoculars with good lenses, the image should be clear, bright, and sharp across the field; that is, it should be in focus from edge to edge, not just in the middle.

It used to be the case that these special coatings were only found on high-end bins, but now you can find them more and more often on good entry-level models. With a little prior research, you should be able to find a pair of quality bins at a very reasonable price.

As I said, cheap binoculars are usually better than nothing at all when you are getting started. If you are going to spend a lot of time looking at birds, however, a cheap pair won't be very satisfying in the long run. It isn't necessary to have the best of the best, though they really are astonishingly good. Think of quality binoculars as an investment in the future. Save up some money, do some research, and you should be able to find something at a price you can afford. And these days, with the advent of Web sites like eBay® and craigslist, you can even hunt for a true bargain in a used pair.

Preparing the Kit

You may choose to get all or only some of the gear I recommended right away. Certainly, however, the very first thing I'd suggest acquiring would be a field notebook. It is inexpensive, easy to carry around, and forms the basis of all of the drawing and obser-vation exercises you'll be doing. After the journal, the next thing I'd strongly suggest in terms of priorities would be a good pair of binoculars. Without them it is virtually impossible to study birds, which you will be doing in order to learn general observation and identification techniques. It could be that you can't afford a good pair at this point, and that's fine. You might be able to borrow some or start out with a less than ideal pair and work your way up. Or, failing either of those possibilities, you could put off that part of the book until later.

In any case, once you have procured your basic field kit, there are still a few things you need to do in order to maximize the utility of your tools.

PREPARING THE JOURNAL
Measuring Scale

There are a few things I like to do to right away with every field notebook I buy. The first of these is to put some sort of scale inside the cover. Often I find a plant or track that I want to make some notes about, and size is one of the more important "field marks" we can use. It is handy to have some way of measuring, and rather than carting around a ruler for this purpose (that easily can be lost), I'll use the scale I've drawn in my notebook. It needn't be fancy—just some marks along one edge that you can place next to the thing you'd like to measure. I like to mark out four to eight inches (depending on the notebook I'm using), with the first two marked in quarters as well.

Beaufort Scale

Weather notes are among those I like to include on a regular basis in my journal entries. In the interest of graceful simplicity, however, I've opted not to carry a bulky weather station with me. Instead, I rely on some of the knowledge about clouds, temperature, and wind direction that I've learned over the years, as well as one or two tricks. For example, since I don't carry an anemometer with me, it is useful to have some other, noninstrumental means of measuring wind speed. Fortunately, there is such a thing, and it's called the Beaufort scale. Named after Admiral Sir Francis Beaufort, it was developed in 1805 to enable sailors to estimate wind speeds based on visual observations. Today, the Beaufort scale has evolved to be used on land as well as sea, using common things you might feel or see around you in order to provide a wind speed estimate. For example, at 4–7 mph, you feel wind on your face and leaves rustle. At 13–18 mph, wind

THE (MODIFIED) BEAUFORT SCALE FOR LAND

Force	Wind Speed (mph)	Description	Observational description
0	0–1	Calm	calm; smoke rises vertically
1	1–3	Light air	smoke drifts slightly
2	4–7	Light breeze	wind felt on face; leaves rustle
3	7–10	Gentle breeze	leaves and small twigs in constant motion; light flag extends
4	13–18	Moderate breeze	dust and loose paper lift; small branches move (close your mouth, or you'll be spitting grit)
5	19–24	Fresh breeze	small, leafed trees sway; crested wavelets form on inland water (time to beach the canoe)
6	25–31	Strong breeze	large branches move; telephone wires whistle
7	32–38	Near gale	entire trees in motion; hard to walk against wind
8	39–46	Gale	twigs and branches break off trees (seek shelter)
9	47–54	Severe gale	slight structural damage occurs; commercial signs rip apart (seek shelter)
10	55–63	Storm	trees uprooted; roofs come off houses (seek shelter)
11	64–72	Violent storm	severe structural damage occurs to houses (seek shelter)
12	73–	Hurricane	pigs finally fly (shelter probably gone)

raises dust and loose paper, and tree branches move. And so on. The scale is measured in "force," with 0 the lowest (calm; smoke rises vertically), and 12 the highest (hurricane). On the opposite page is my own version of the original, slightly modified to fit my locale and needs. (For example, I don't see a lot of chimney pots around here, the uprooting of which marked 47–54 mph winds, and waving grasses are more properly found in the prairie than are trees.) If you want to see the original Beaufort scale, there are several sources available online.

Although I've lived most of my life in places that have a lot of wind and have gotten pretty good at estimating wind speed by virtue of being exposed to it most of the time, I still like to paste a small copy of the Beaufort scale on one of the inside covers of my journal. It's a handy little reference to have when I want to check my estimate against a known scale. If you'd like to do the same, you could copy this one and paste it in your journal. It will fit in the Strathmore sketchbook, but for smaller journals, you may have to find a copy machine and reduce it in size.

Sketch Frames

There is one other thing I like to do to prepare my notebook for field drawing. Although I don't like to draw on small pages, I do like to put many of my sketches inside frames on the page. So before I go out into the field, I cut two or three squares and rectangles out of stiff paper. These don't have to be very big—something two or three inches on any given side will do the trick. You could even follow the lead of one of my students, Monica Warren, and use those otherwise useless fake credit cards that come as advertisements in junk mail. I'll show you how and why to use the frames in the chapter on Field Drawing. For now, simply procure a couple and have them ready to go.

To hold my frames, I like to make a pocket that I paste in the back of the notebook. A heavy envelope cut in half, stuck on the inside back cover with a little glue, does the trick neatly. The pocket is also useful for small, loose bits of paper you might like to keep with your journal.

Here is an example of the front of a notebook belonging to a former student of mine, Monica Warren, in which you can see how she has incorporated each of the elements described on the previous page.

Monica R. Warren

FOR EACH DAILY LOG INCLUDE:
1. Location
2. Time
3. Temperature / Weather
4. Wind Conditions
5. Map
6. North Arrow

North Arrows:

100 meters = 65 paces
1 pace = 1.539 meters
1 meter = .65 pace

The inside back cover of Monica's notebook includes the Beaufort scale and ruler measurements in both inches and centimeters.

The Beaufort Scale for Land

Force	Wind Speed (mph)	Description	Observational description
0	0-1	Calm	calm; smoke rises vertically
1	1-3	Light air	smoke drifts slightly (why are you smoking?)
2	4-7	Light breeze	wind felt on face; leaves rustle
3	7-10	Gentle breeze	leaves and small twigs in constant motion; light fla extends
4	13-18	Moderate breeze	dust and loose paper lift; small branches move (c your mouth, or you'll be spitting grit)
5	19-24	Fresh breeze	small, leafed trees sway; crested wavelets form o inland water (time to beach the canoe)
6	25-31	Strong breeze	large branches move; telephone wires whistle
7	32-38	Near gale	entire trees in motion; hard to walk against wind
8	39-46	Gale	twigs and branches break off trees (seek shelter)
9	47-54	Severe gale	slight structural damage occurs; commercial sign apart (especially if they are advertising auto part' (seek shelter)
10	55-63	Storm	trees uprooted; roofs come off houses (seek shelt
11	64-72	Violent storm	severe structural damage occurs to houses (seek shelter)
12	73-	Hurricane	Pigs finally fly (shelter probably gone)

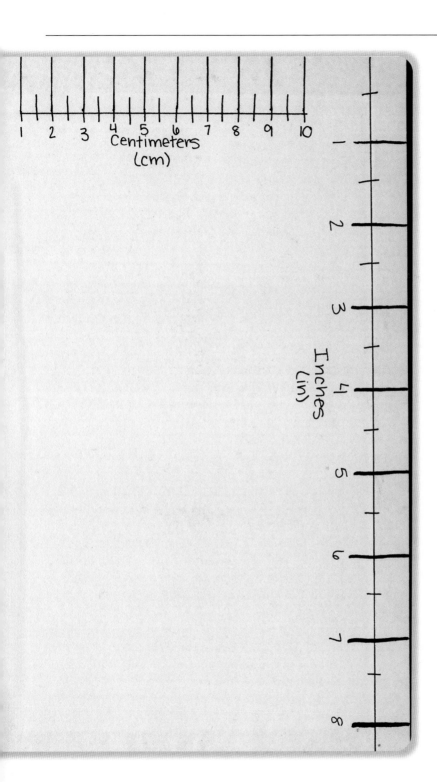

Centimeters
(cm)

Inches
(in)

PREPARING TO USE YOUR BINOCULARS
Eyecups
Although binoculars are pretty simple to use, there are a couple of things that you need to do to "fit" them to your eyes. To start, if you wear eyeglasses, I'll assume you've done your homework and acquired a pair of bins that has long eye relief. If so, you'll still need to lower the eyecups so that your glasses can get as close to the surface of the ocular as possible. On some models, this is accomplished by rolling the flexible rubber eyecups down. On many newer models, you can twist the eyecups down to their lowest position. In either case, the effect is to enlarge the circle of view that you see when you look through the oculars.

If you don't wear glasses, simply leave the eyecups fully extended. If you're like me and wear sunglasses some but not all of the time, you'll probably want to purchase a pair of bins that have the twist feature; it makes going back and forth between glasses (eyecups down) and no glasses (eyecups up) easier.

Adjusting Interpupillary Distance
Now look through the binoculars. You should see either two circles or one pointed ellipse. Push the barrels of the bins inward or pull outward until you get a single, more or less round "circle of view."

Diopter Adjustment
The binoculars can now be set to focus for each of your eyes. On one of the oculars (nearly always the right one), you'll find a set of tick marks. Gently try twisting this eyepiece to see if it turns. If it does, that is your diopter adjustment. On some binoculars, however, the diopter adjustment is not on either of the eyepieces, though the adjustment mechanism still corresponds to only one ocular. This is the case with a pair of Swarovskis I used to own, in which the diopter adjustment was found on the center axis, but it was used to adjust the binoculars to my right eye.

Once you have found the diopter adjustment, look through the binoculars at something that has a crisp edge, like the rough bark of a tree or a telephone wire. Close your right eye (or the one that corresponds to the diopter adjuster), and focus on the crisp edge using just your left eye and turning the primary focus wheel. Once the edge is in focus, close your left eye, and turn the diopter adjustment to bring the image into focus for your right eye.

When you open both eyes, the image should be sharp and clear. Look at the tick marks on your diopter adjustment; you should be able to see that it has moved in either a + or – direction away from the main registration mark. Make note of how far to one side or the other it has moved and remember it. Sometimes your bins will get knocked around and your diopter will shift, or you'll loan them to someone who knows how to use binoculars (and who will adjust them to his or her own eyes accordingly). A quick glance at the tick marks will tell you if you need to put them right again.

To underscore this last point, on more than one occasion, I've looked through my binoculars and been dismayed at how smudgy and filmy the image is. "I really need to clean these bins!" I'll cry. Then it occurs to me to look at the diopter setting. Sure enough, the ocular has shifted out of focus.

Binocular Technique

Although they're simple to use, binoculars are like any other instrument—we're not born knowing the best techniques. I am reminded of this every time I watch new birders struggle to locate a bird in a tree. They can see the bird with their eyes, but when they raise the bins for a look, the bird seems to have mysteriously vanished. With a little tweaking and practice, however, even novice birders can master, in the space of a few minutes, the skill of putting birds (or other objects) in their circle of view—most of the time. (I add "most of the time" as a caveat because birds and animals often move around, making the task of locating them in your binoculars more of an art than a skill. This is especially true of warblers and kinglets.)

The easiest way to learn to find things in your circle of view is to start by practicing on an inanimate object, such as a flower or the top of a fence post. Stare at the object, then, *without taking your eyes off it,* lift the binoculars and look through them. The object should be somewhere in your circle of view, preferably in the center. Practice on the same object a couple of times, and then move on to a tree. Find a small object there (this could be a sitting bird), stare at it, and lift the binoculars without moving your head or eyes. The object should be in the circle of view. It's as simple as that.

The real trick, as I've said, is locating the subjects that move around quite a bit. You can get good at this, too, with a little practice. Just remember that the key is to locate the subject first, then *quickly and smoothly* raise the bins without moving your head or eyes. It doesn't work every time, but it works often enough that most of your birding experiences will be happy ones.

Finally, it should go without saying (though I'll say it here) that *you should never look directly at the sun with your binoculars. Doing so can blind you.* So I make a point of always being aware of where the sun is in the sky. That way, if I happen to be tracking a hawk in flight and I know its path will lead across the vicinity of the sun, I lower my bins and enjoy the view with my very own God-given eyes. That's good enough for me.

Hand Lens and Pocket Magnifier Technique

I've found that the simplest way to use a hand lens or pocket magnifier is to bring it close to one eye and move the object you are trying to inspect in and out until it comes into focus. This seems to work a little better for me than holding the hand lens away from my eyes and moving it back and forth to focus. Try it both ways, however, and find the one that works best for you.

These items represent my bare-bones field kit—something I have lying around the house ready to go whenever I get the impulse to "be there." Its purpose is simply to provide me with the tools I need to observe and record what I see when I venture out into the field. You may find, with a little experimentation, that there are some items you don't need and others you'd like to add. For example, you might decide that you never use a hand lens or compass. Or you might find that you'd prefer a real watercolor set, which in turn might require a bigger field bag. Over time, the field kit will become as personalized as your experiences with nature, and that's part of what it's all about. The opinions about the gear are solely my own, and they are simply suggestions for getting started. There is only one opinion that I'll stand by firmly, and that is the one that opened this chapter, from Greg Brown's song "Two Little Feet": "stuff with no knowledge is never enough."

That's what the rest of the book is about.

2. Field Sketching: Basic Skills

Many people are intimidated by the idea of drawing,[1] even if it is something that they are doing just for themselves, in a journal that no one else will ever see. Somewhere in their childhood they got the notion that they weren't good at it. Maybe their horses looked like ducks or their trees looked like houses. Or maybe, like me, their teachers always chose to hang someone else's drawing on the classroom wall because, unlike their classmates, they insisted on coloring yellow raincoats red and blue skies a streaky purple. Whatever

Carolina wren

I look; morning to night I am never done with looking. Looking I mean not just standing around, but standing around as though with your arms open.

—Mary Oliver, "Where Does the Temple Begin, Where Does It End?"

---

1. In this book, "drawing" and "sketching" will be used interchangeably.

the reason, if you have avoided drawing what you see in the natural world because you have felt embarrassed or frustrated by your efforts in the past, it's time to give it another try.

Every year, I have students who start my course by telling me that they have no talent for drawing. I'm not really sure what talent is, though I'm sure some people do indeed have it. Few people would ever walk up to a piano and think they could play a concerto having never had a single lesson, yet they expect that they should be able to draw a subject with skill (what artists call "rendering") without ever first learning how. In the same way that most of us can learn to bang out some tunes with a few lessons and some practice, nearly everyone can learn to render a subject in a way that is satisfying. It just takes learning a few basic skills and committing to practice.

But why bother? Why not just take a picture? It's certainly easy enough to do with a cell phone or small digital camera—a press of a button and you've recorded a flower you want to identify. And if you're really serious about photography, you're probably already out in the field "chasing good light" for a maximum visual effect. Either way, incorporating photos can be a very nice aesthetic addition to your notebook. But drawing and sketching force you to slow down and study a subject in a way that photography does not. Taking the time to draw something in your journal—*even if you think you have no talent for it*—helps you, as Mary Oliver suggests in her poem on the previous page, look at the natural world as if your arms are wide open to what it has to offer.

Some of you are saying now, "That's all well and good, but I really *can't* draw! This approach simply will not work for me." (I know you are saying it because I hear it all the time.)

First of all, this is not about creating a work of art—it is about taking a good look at something. So stop putting a lot of pressure on yourself about what the final product is going to look like, and relax and learn to enjoy the *process*.

Second, in spite of what you might presently believe, sketching a respectable facsimile of something is really very easy when it's broken down into specific steps. Together we are going to walk through some simple, progressive exercises so that you can understand how to make your hand draw what your eye (and mind) sees. If you follow them faithfully and *practice* (remember those scales!), you'll be surprised at how much you improve in a very short time.

These are exercises I use in my classes, and it may seem at times as though some of them are overly simplistic. You can, of course, choose to skip some of them, particularly if you have some drawing or painting background. But remember, they're progressive—there's a reason for doing them this way, so I encourage you to do them in the order presented. The first exercises take no more than a few seconds to a couple of minutes to do; so even though you may think at first glance that some of them are so simple as to be silly, take the time to do them and try to do each as well as you can. Take the Soto Zen approach: relax and trust that the *path* is the enlightenment. If the exercise is to draw a circle, enjoy the process of drawing a near-perfect circle. Don't rush it—draw as if you have a lifetime to complete your sketch. Finally, when you begin to get tired or frustrated, put the work away for a while. Come back to it when you're feeling mellow and ready to spend some time noodling around.

In all of the sections, you'll notice that I focus a lot on birds, though I also incorporate other aspects of nature, such as landscapes and plants. Birds are what I know and love best, so I tend to draw and study them more than other things. Of course, you are not restricted only to their study, but the tricks for rendering birds are pretty much the same as for everything else—if you learn their secrets, you've unlocked the secrets of drawing in general.

STEP 1: DRAWING SIMPLE SHAPES
Everything in nature can be broken down into the following simple two-dimensional shapes that we all can draw: square, rectangle, circle, ellipse, and triangle.

Basic Drawing Skills

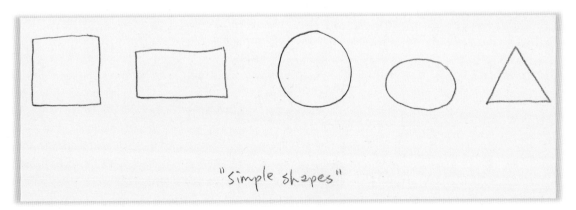

"Simple shapes"

That's it. If you look at any object, you should be able to see that it is either one of these shapes or some combination of them. Just for fun, let's examine our first object of nature: a sausage. (Okay, I realize that, strictly speaking, a sausage is not part of nature. Let's just say that it's a sausage I'm eating while on a picnic.)

The sausage, as you can see, is really just two circles and a slightly curved rectangle. There's nothing hard about it.

If you think a sausage is a silly thing with which to start, take a look at the sketch below where, with the addition of just a few other simple shapes and marks, our saucy little wurst is turned into a squirrel.

Learning to pick out the simple shapes in objects will take you a long way toward being able to draw what your eyes and mind see.

Sketching out the shapes first will help you to render things in their proper proportions. All too often we start drawing something at one end and continue straight through to the other, only to find that we've created some-

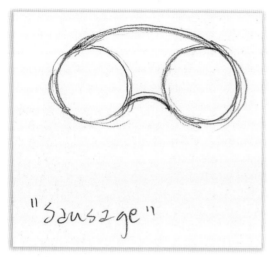

"Sausage"

thing that is all out of whack. If you look at the drawings of old masters, however, you occasionally can see the broad traces of shapes, just like the ones you've drawn. So you see, even geniuses use this technique to start their drawings!

Below are some more sketches of the squirrels in my backyard. These guys clamber around by the dozens in the pecan trees outside my studio and make great practice subjects. I've left my initial sketches of the simple shapes in so that you can see the way they form the starting point for each squirrel.

There are other ways to combine these simple shapes, of course. Two ellipses and a rectangle make a cylinder, an ellipse and a triangle form a cone, and so on. On the next page are just a few examples of how you can combine these to form shapes that are more three-dimensional. If you look closely, you can see the faint marks of circles and ellipses I used to sketch in the basic shapes.

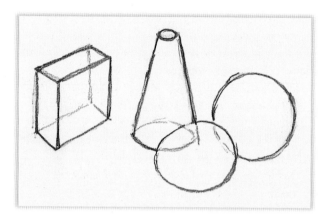

one mug, ready for Morning tea . . .

Don't just look for the two-dimensional simple shapes— check out combinations of them, too, in the things you want to draw. To the left is an example of how you can combine shapes to draw an ordinary object you probably have lying around, such as a mug of tea.

Notice in this sketch that the sides of the mug, which are vertical in real life, are also vertical on the page. A common mistake that students make is to draw vertical lines at a slant on the page, causing the object to look as if it is tilting.

Often a student will tell me that she can't draw a near-perfect circle or square. I respond that neither can I—at least, not on the first pass. What I can do is correct a shape as I go along and "sneak up" on perfection. That is, I'm not afraid to change a line until I get it right. Here is an example of what I'm talking about:

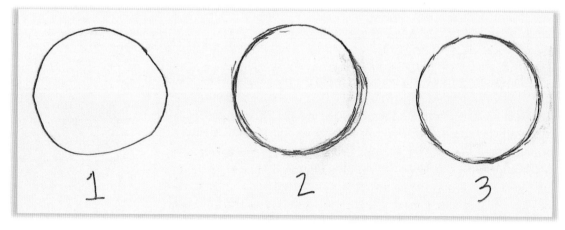

Spending time on trying to create a perfect circle is not wasted. Practicing this is like practicing scales in music. It trains your eye to see what needs to be corrected in a drawing and improves the manual dexterity of your hand, which are key elements in making an image look the way you want it to.

When a student tells me he can't make his hand do what his brain sees, we analyze it together. If I ask him to show me a spot in his drawing that doesn't look right, he is able to point it out. Then I'll ask him what is wrong with it, and he'll respond that the foot on the bird seems small or the bill looks too long. At that I suggest he change it by making the foot bigger or the bill shorter. We go back and forth on the drawing like this, sneaking up on perfection, until at long last he arrives at a very satisfactory result.

EXERCISES

1. With your mechanical pencil, practice drawing circles, triangles, and rectangles for a few minutes. Try very hard to make the shapes look as perfect as you can—don't be afraid to change a line you've made. If your circle looks more like an egg than a circle, shave off the bits that stick out and round out the flat parts a tad. Keep at it until the shape is a near-perfect circle.

   Hold the pencil as you would normally for writing, but remember, this is supposed to be relaxing, so take a deep breath and loosen up that death grip.

2. After you have some satisfactory circles, triangles, and rectangles, try putting them together to form slightly more complex shapes, such as the sausage or tea mug on the previous page.

If I had to pick only one thing to tell you about learning to draw, it would be this: *If you can see what is wrong with an image, you can correct it.*

Practicing these simple skills will help you see how to continually correct things until you get them right. Once you've done this for a while, though, it's good to move on to "real" subjects. Pick four or five inanimate objects in which you can see the simple shapes and draw these, working on them until you feel you have the shapes and proportions right, exactly as you worked on drawing the perfect circle.

STEP 2: PROPORTION

Of course, it doesn't do us any good to pick out the simple shapes in a subject and draw them if we don't keep in mind their relationship to the *overall* size and shape. For example, I wouldn't want my squirrels to have heads that are too little for their bodies or arms that are too big. So while I'm sketching in the rough shapes, I need to pay attention to their proportions—how big or small they are in relation to the rest of the subject.

Keeping things proportional is not really that hard once you make yourself aware of it. The quickest and easiest method for keeping a proportional relationship between parts of a whole is to estimate the size of something by comparing it with another component of the subject. For example, when my cat Koho is stretched out, his head is about one-fourth the length of his body.

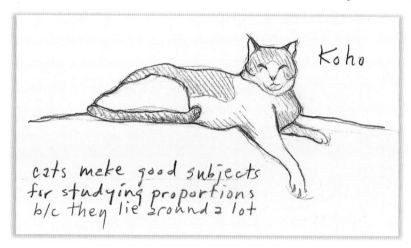

Koho

cats make good subjects
for studying proportions
b/c they lie around a lot

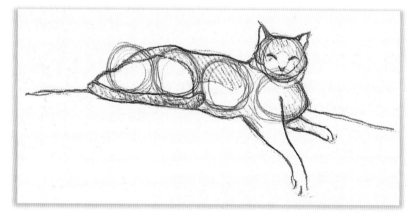

Another approach is to divide the subject into rough grids, as shown in the illustration of the bird's head in different poses on the opposite page. This technique for placing a bird's eye in the right spot is one I learned from noted bird artist John Sill. Sill divides the head into horizontal and vertical grids, and then draws the eye just above the "equatorial" line and just behind the first "longitudinal" line. This generic diagram will serve when rendering most birds. Here I provide my slightly modified version of the full diagram Sill uses for establishing the generic configuration of a bird, as well as a three-dimensional interpretation. Details will differ, of course, among different families, genera, and even species, but this is a very good place to start.

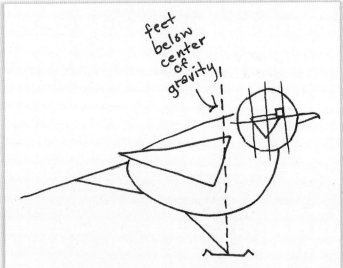

feet below center of gravity

Artists and their works were once a very important part of the study of natural history, and some would argue that they are just as important today. The very best field guides have paintings and drawings instead of photographs. There is a good reason for this. The artist controls the image, and, rather than being dependent on fortuitous lighting and angles, he or she can render a more "true" portrait of a subject. I like to imagine that when I am sketching in my journal, I am walking in the footsteps of a long line of naturalists/artists.

EXERCISE

Find four or five subjects and practice getting the proportions right. Remember to use simple shapes and grid lines to figure out where to place features.

A "Bird" for Practice

To help students see the shapes in subjects in a way that is dynamic instead of lifeless, I created a bird out of a Styrofoam egg and sphere that are connected with a pipe cleaner. For a tail, I used a small cone-shaped piece of plastic that is normally used to hold a flower stem in floral arrangements (these can be found in a craft store, but any similarly sized cone or wedge shape will do), and for the legs and bill, I used thin dowels. I marked a grid on the head to show where to place the eyes. I shaved off part of the egg so that the head can sit more on the shoulders. The result looks like this:

Here are some more examples, drawn by a student of mine, Katy Watson. As you can see, these are meant to be done very quickly. The idea is to get a feel for the movement that exists between the shapes.

STEP 3: SHADING AND TONAL VALUES

Thankfully, we live in a world of light and shadow. If it were not so, things would look especially, well, two-dimensional to our eyes. In the drawing below, I've taken the same simple shapes and added light and dark values. When you compare them with the line drawings of the same shapes, they seem to pop out of the page a bit more—in other words, I've added another dimension.

To make these, I bought some Styrofoam shapes at a local crafts store and directed a strong lamp to shine on them at a sharp angle. This is something you can do for very little cost, and it's a great way to practice shading techniques. However, you can also search around your home and find similar practice shapes.

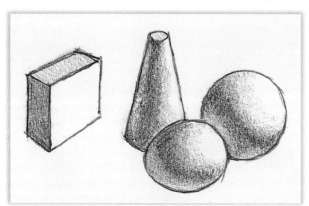

I've left the shadows cast by the shapes out of the drawing so that you can see the effects of direct light on the shapes themselves more clearly. We'll cover cast shadows in the section on perspective. Notice that the shadows on the objects themselves are actually somewhat complex; that is, there are places where light is reflected from the surface on which they are sitting, as well as from other objects.

I made the drawing above using a number 2B pencil (see chapter one for an explanation of pencil hardness numbers). When you are using ink to make your drawings and sketches, however, it is sometimes more effective to use other techniques to establish tonal values, such as the hachure or "hatch" marks to the left.

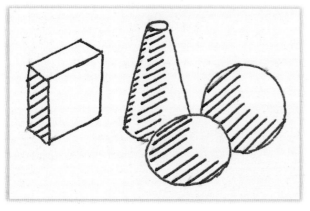

I think these hachure marks are a handy way to explore the shapes of values on objects and the way those shapes create three dimensions. There are many such techniques for ink drawing. We won't go into them here, but there is a list of suggested reading at the end of this book in which you can find some further instruction on this and other topics.

In these drawings of geese, I demonstrate how all of these components—from the initial simple shapes through tonal values and cast shadows—are put together to create a completed sketch.

cacklers & canadas '05 TOMLINSON

EXERCISES

1. Find some simple, three-dimensional objects and a strong lamp. Put the two together and examine the results. Notice that the darkest part of the shadow and the lightest part of the highlight may not always be where you expect them. For example, on the cone in my sketch on page 34, there was a back-highlight on one edge so that the darkest part of the shadow was actually more toward the middle. Use your 2B (soft lead) pencil to sketch in the shapes of the shadows on your objects.

2. Make five sketches of the shadows on objects using pencil and five more using ink.

Drawing Wild Subjects: Getting Started

Now that we've "practiced our scales," it's time to move on to wild subjects. Wild animal subjects are sometimes hard to learn to draw simply because they don't stay still long enough for us to study them as we are sketching. Birds are an excellent example of this. Some species, like egrets, are somewhat cooperative, as they don't tend to move very quickly or often. Others, like warblers and wrens, can be maddening to try to study since, besides being small, they are often very busy birds.

Drawing most birds in the field is, in fact, very difficult to do. Most finished drawings and paintings of birds have used a variety of sources of image information, including field sketches, photos, drawings in field guides, and so on. If you want to learn how to quickly sketch birds (or other wildlife) in the field, your best chance is to first learn how to draw them quickly in the studio. One of the best ways to practice this is to draw from a photo image.[2]

Drawing from photos accomplishes two things. First, it burns a template into your skills. That is, in the same way shooting a basketball over and over creates muscle memory, so does drawing the same subject in many different poses. By drawing from a photograph, you are not under any pressure to hurry up before the bird flies away, so you can take your time to study it—the way it hunches when it is cold, the way it tucks its head to preen, the way it scrapes its bill against a tree branch. After a while, your drawing muscles come to form a memory of how to sketch birds so that when you are sketching a living subject you can do it quickly and surely—you have a memory template from which to draw.

2. One word of caution: All the photo images you find in books and magazines are protected by copyright, and it is a violation to copy a photo to create an image for sale. However, it is probably okay to use the photos for your personal practice exercises. Also, using photos as reference (that is, checking to see what a particular feature looks like) in creating your own original work is permissible.

The second good thing about drawing from photos is that it's a good way to warm up your skills. Instead of sitting down and drawing a living subject cold, you can limber up those drawing muscles on a sketch that doesn't "count." After two or three of these, you can tackle the real thing with ease.

To get started, find yourself two or three photos of a bird you commonly see in your backyard. You want to choose photos of a local bird rather than an exotic bird (a resplendent quetzal, for example) since part of the purpose of this exercise is to build that muscle memory and move on to practicing on a live subject. Now, put on some music or slip a movie in the DVD player, brew yourself a little soothing green tea and honey, gather up your pencils and paper, and sit back and relax. Commence to draw. Take your time.

One thing that can help you learn to look at proportions is to divide your image into a grid, noting which parts of the bird or birds fall into each section, as in this example of a white-winged dove.

Now identify the simple shapes and sketch them in first. Then add some details, a few at a time.

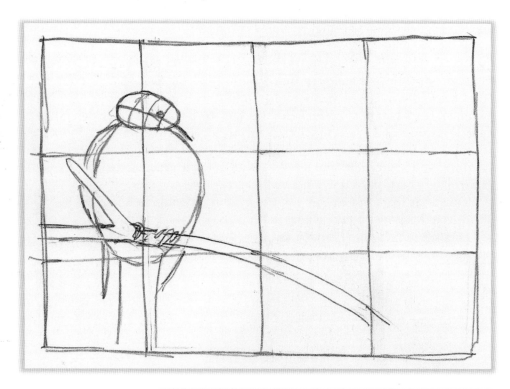

If you have trouble with something—the angle of a bill, for example—reduce it to its simple shape and draw it in three dimensions. It is not a bill on a head; it is a small shape on a sphere, as in this example of an unusual yellow house finch.

Here's a slightly different example, this time of an evening grosbeak with an open bill. Again, if you reduce the bill to simple shapes, it doesn't have to be intimidating at all.

Try to capture the attitude of the subject. Is the head cocked because it hears something? Is it hunched against the winter cold? Draw the simple shapes of the head and body as they relate to each other in these attitudes, as in this example of a male house finch waiting in line at the feeder.

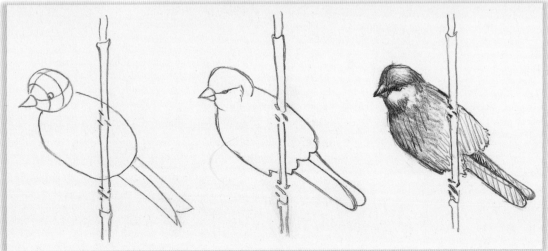

Build a Feeding Station

Learning to draw birds can be especially frustrating because they tend not to stay still for any length of time. Still, if you can learn to draw this moving target, you can do it for almost anything. If you have a backyard, it is easy to set it up to be a sort  of training ground for practicing these tough subjects. Find a spot to create a feeding station with different types of feeders and food to attract different species. In my own feeding station, I have a couple of tube feeders, one for thistle seeds for finches and the other for sunflowers seeds for other perching birds, and a platform feeder for birds that normally feed on the ground. These options cover nearly all the seed-eating birds that might visit my garden. I also have a small basin for water. Both the food and water are placed away from shrubs or any other cover that might hide a cat or other predator.

It is optimal if the feeding station can be viewed from numerous vantage points. I can see mine from several different windows in my house, including my upstairs studio, as well as from strategic places in the garden itself. To facilitate the latter, I've even built a viewing blind that I move around to get the best light for taking photographs.

In doing these photo studies, your goal is not to create a finished drawing so much as it is to learn to sketch a small bird quickly, over and over, in several different poses. In time, you'll leave off the grid overlying the photo and sketch without it. The same will be true of the grid you use overlying the head, since once you master drawing birds quickly, you'll have a sense of what a bird looks like without even having to look at a model. This is important because you'll be able to study a bird while it is before you, and then draw it while it's still fresh in your mind if it flies away. You'll be able to do the same when out in the field or looking through your window at the birds around your feeder.

In addition to the "quick and dirty" method of using photos, I have three feeders and several pecan trees right outside my studio windows. My studio is on the second floor, so I am eye level with all the busy workings in the pecans. I keep a digital camera handy and routinely take some shots expressly for the purpose of stretching my drawing skills. I'm not trying to create great bird photographs here—that's another skill altogether. These photos are merely an opportunity to study birds and other subjects at my leisure.

I keep a spotting scope set up at one of my studio windows for the same purpose—to practice sketching what I see. Only with the spotting scope there's no freezing the action, so one of the things I work on when I use it is the ability to sketch quickly. This is easier to do with a living subject (as opposed to a photo) because movement sometimes makes it possible to see more than if the animal were frozen in one position.

Now we can put together all the things we've learned and begin to draw in the field—which is what we have been working toward all along. Following is a page from one of my journals showing some very simple sketches, quickly done, of the birds around my feeder on a cold winter day, as seen through my spotting scope. By now you should be able to see how I've used each of the exercises to arrive at these field sketches.

EXERCISES: Suggested Follow-Up

1. Try the sausage trick on other things besides squirrels. This exercise can be done indoors or out, but wherever you choose to try it, be sure to make yourself comfortable so that you can spend a few minutes of relaxed drawing. Once you're settled, pick an object that interests you. Start with something easy for this first exercise; after you feel like you've drawn a reasonable leaf, coffee mug, or tree, you can move on to more complex combinations of shapes, such as a cat, flower head, or bird.

   Don't worry about shading or making the sketch look finished. Don't even worry too much about making your objects three-dimensional. The goal here is to train your eyes to see the simple shapes that make up complex forms, so concentrate on that for now. Make a total of ten simple drawings of ten objects.

2. Buy a magazine for birders. Pick out five or six photographs of birds and sketch them, paying close attention to the simple shapes.

3. Make five sketches each day for a week. Pick any subject you wish (though I'd stay away from complex combinations like landscapes at the start—you can eventually work up to that). Be sure to leave the traces of your simple shapes in your final drawing.

4. Construct your own Styrofoam bird. Draw it in several different poses, from different perspectives.

The instruction in this chapter is really all you need to get started on your field sketches. There are other techniques you can add to your repertoire that will further improve the quality of your drawings; these will be covered in the following chapter. I also include some suggestions for how to compose your entries in the journal to maximize the aesthetic effect, though as I said in the introduction to this chapter, creating "art" is not the reason for learning to sketch the natural world. Doing a few simple things to make your journal pages more attractive, however, can deepen your enjoyment of the process.

3. Field Sketching: Beyond the Basics

What cooks mean with the phrase to the right is that how food looks sharpens our appetite for the dish (or dulls it, for that matter). What good cooks also know is that just a little bit of color, texture, and attention to arrangement on the plate (all of which is called "presentation") can go a long way toward taking a dish from bland to enticing. Consider cookbooks, for example. Which one would you be more likely to pick out in a bookstore—one with lavish,

Green clouds
View at dinnertime

mouth-watering color photos next to the recipes or one with the same recipes, but without any photos?

The same is true for your journal. It isn't strictly necessary to do so, but making your journal a feast for the eyes can only serve to enhance your enjoyment of it. And it doesn't take much to accomplish this—as with food, a little attention to color, texture, and arrangement can do a lot.

The artist Georgia O'Keefe believed that visual aesthetics were so vital to the richness of life that even the manner in which a stamp was placed on an envelope was important. In the same way, we can enhance the richness of the journaling experience if we take some care with our entries. This is not to say that every page of your field notebook will be a work of art in miniature—such thinking, in fact, is certain to bring a kind of anxiety to your journaling efforts. The notebook should be a place where you feel free to experiment, learn new techniques, and verbally ruminate without worrying about spelling or proper essay form. It should, and often does, look like a collection of stops and starts. In other words, it is a place for practice and data- and idea-gathering—a perpetual work in progress, not a finished product. Too much concern about how it looks will only inhibit your creativity. My own journal, in fact, is filled with many such pages of random, unformed thoughts and creaky sketches, and very few of the pages, if any, would be worth hanging on the wall. Even so, I want my journal to be something I enjoy opening and browsing, and if it is pleasing to my eyes, so much the better.

Making it visually presentable, or even attractive, is not all that hard, and there are a few tips I can offer to help you do so. You won't want to do this for every entry you make, since it won't always be appropriate—as I said, the journal should be a place of practice and note-taking, not a finished work of art. But if you make a point now and then to create a beautiful page, it will pay off when you look at the *whole* of the journal.

Color and Line

COLOR

One of the simplest things you can do to spice up your journal is to add color. A little restraint, however, is often preferable to a lot of heavily applied, indiscriminately used color. I find that too much color can leave my journal page looking garish and unfocused. A dab or two in the right place, however, can make the page "pop." Rather than worry about coloring the whole bird or flower, you might simply apply a tint of color where you want to emphasize something. As an example, look at the little sketch that opened this chapter. One early evening, while cooking at a campsite on a canoe trip in the Boundary Waters Canoe Area Wilderness in Minnesota, I was struck by the rich but gentle colors in the trees across the lake. A quick sketch (note the simple shapes) and a light hand with the watercolor pencils was all I needed to capture my impression of the moment.

This sketch of a Cassin's finch is another example of how a little color can be useful, in this case, for the purposes of identification.

In particular, if you use watercolor pencils, you probably want to apply the color sparingly—with these tools, too much pigment can lead to a rather muddy-looking final product when you add the water. Start gently and practice a bit, and you will soon find the right amount for your taste.

EXERCISE: Using Watercolor Pencils

I have my students do the following exercise to get a feel for their illustration tools. We use watercolor pencils, but it can be adapted for your medium of choice. The exercise gives you a feel for both for how much pigment to apply and how different colors go together. Start by drawing a line horizontally through the middle of a page in your journal, then fill the top half with small boxes (we'll talk about what to do with the bottom half in a moment). Take a couple of your favorite colors and fill the top row of boxes, going from dark to light in each, like this:

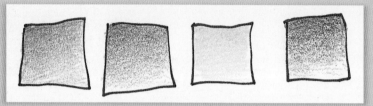

This will help you see how much pressure to apply to achieve the effect you want for intensity of color. (Hint: Always start light and go darker—it is easier to put color on than it is to take it off. Also, if you are having trouble telling whether your gradient is uniform, try squinting your eyes when you look at it.)

Next, take a single color and fill three or four boxes with a uniform amount of pigment, but make each box a different intensity. Now take your watercolor brush, wet it thoroughly, and tap it against the side of your water container to get rid of any excess. Use your brush to apply a dab of water to one half of each of the boxes. This will show you how water reacts to different amounts of pigment.

Finally, fill the remainder of the boxes with circles and start combining colors to see how they look next to each other, like this:

The top half of your page is now a template for the effects of your watercolor pencils and should look something like this:

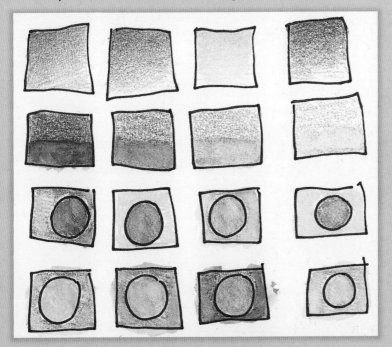

You will probably like some of the boxes more than others—that's okay. The point of the exercise is to practice so that you can see how much pigment and water to apply to your sketches.

LINE

In the same way that your sketches can find life through a little color, so too can you improve them by playing with "line." Often, our tendency is to draw all of our lines with the same uniform intensity. The effect is something like an outline. Here is a drawing made at the beginning of a semester in a course I teach on natural history illustration. The student, Jessica Meixner, has graciously allowed me to show it as well as the drawings she made just a couple of months later to illustrate what attention to line intensity can do for your work.

Cardinalis cardinalis
Jessica Meixner

EXERCISE: *Line Intensity*

Here is an exercise to help you develop a feel for line. On the bottom half of the journal page on which you created the boxes of color, draw a series of lines, pressing hard with your pencil, then easing up, and then pressing hard again, over and over. Hold your pencil loosely and allow it to twist this way and that. The result should look something like the picture to the right.

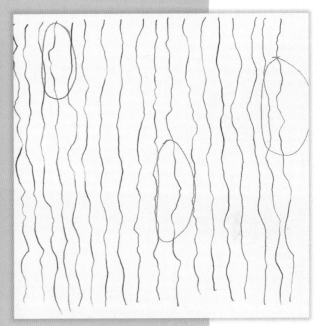

When you are finished with the page, take a moment to examine each line. Select three areas that are particularly appealing to you. You don't have to know why they are appealing—this just helps you get into the habit of appreciating good, elegant lines, the better to create your own when you make your sketches.

In the drawing on the opposite page, the outline effect is created by having a more or less uniform intensity of line.

In this second drawing, the work is much more lively and expressive, due in part to the variation in line intensity. That is, it no longer looks "outliney."

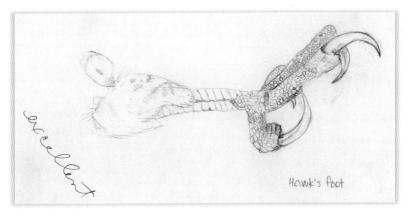

Hawk's foot

Here is what Jessica's final bird anatomy study looked like. I include it to show you that in a very short time span (less than two months in this case), with practice and attention to detail, there can be great improvement in your skills.

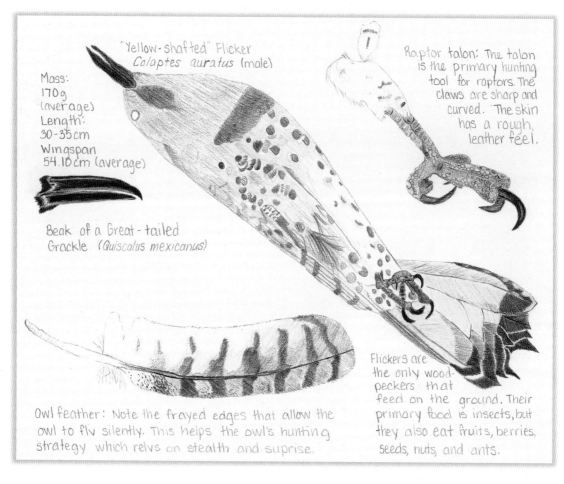

"Yellow-shafted" Flicker
Colaptes auratus (male)

Mass:
170g
(average)
Length:
30-35cm
Wingspan
54.10cm (average)

Beak of a Great-tailed
Grackle *(Quiscalus mexicanus)*

Raptor talon: The talon is the primary hunting tool for raptors. The claws are sharp and curved. The skin has a rough, leather feel.

Owl feather: Note the frayed edges that allow the owl to fly silently. This helps the owl's hunting strategy which relys on stealth and suprise.

Flickers are the only woodpeckers that feed on the ground. Their primary food is insects, but they also eat fruits, berries, seeds, nuts, and ants.

As you sketch in your journal, try to consciously play with line intensity. Make some parts of the line dark and thick and others light and thin. It takes practice and experience to know when to do each, but what you are most interested in is avoiding "sameness." To help develop a feel for this, practice a lot and study the works of others. When you see a sketch you particularly like, look closely at how the artist used variation in line intensity to create expressiveness.

Layout

Just as color and line can be used to make your journal page more visually appealing, how you arrange the material on your page can do the same. Here are a few tips for composing your journal pages for maximum effect.

FILL THE PAGE

Too often, when my students are first starting out, they have a tendency to put one small, lonely image on a page. The result is a series of nearly empty pages, lending the journal an air of half-heartedness—it looks as if the author/artist simply wasn't interested enough in the subject at hand to have anything much to say about it. I'm not sure why there is a tendency for beginning students to do this—perhaps it is simply that they are not used to the concept of practicing their sketches and note-taking, and they subconsciously treat each effort as if it were a single drawing to be handed in on its own sheet of paper. One of the most effective things you can do to enhance the aesthetic appeal of your journal is to make sure you fill the pages; in fact, I find that the journals I enjoy looking at the most are the ones with pages that are chock-full to the brim with writing and sketching. A full page is a lively page. I admit that my own journals do not have as many full pages as I'd like—my students tend to do a better job of this than I. The following pages show three stylistically different examples of journal pages, but I find them all very aesthetically pleasing, in part because they are filled to the brim with work.

Pages from Delilah Clark's journal.

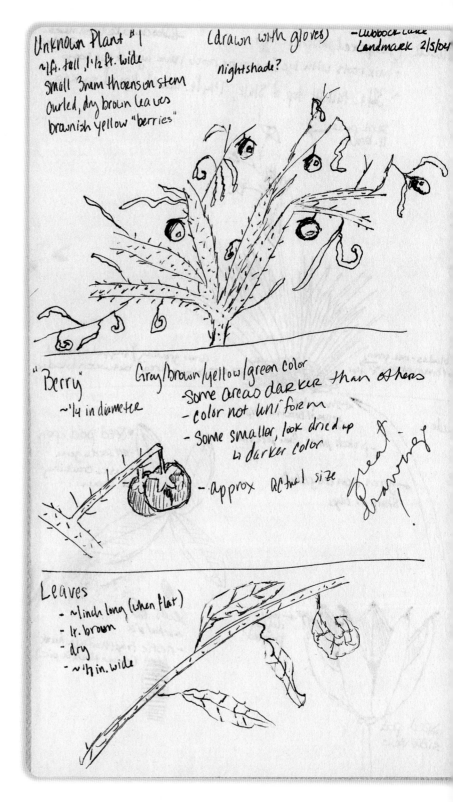

Unknown Plant #1   (drawn with gloves)   —Lubbock Lake
~1ft. tall, 1½ ft. wide   Landmark 2/5/04
small 3mm thorns on stem   nightshade?
Curled, dry brown leaves
brownish yellow "berries"

"Berry"   Gray/brown/yellow/green color
   ~¼ in diameter   -Some areas darker than others
                    - color not uniform
                    - Some smaller, look dried up
                        ↳ darker color

                    -approx actual size   great drawing!

Leaves
   - ~1 inch long (when flat)
   - lt. brown
   - dry
   - ~½ in. wide

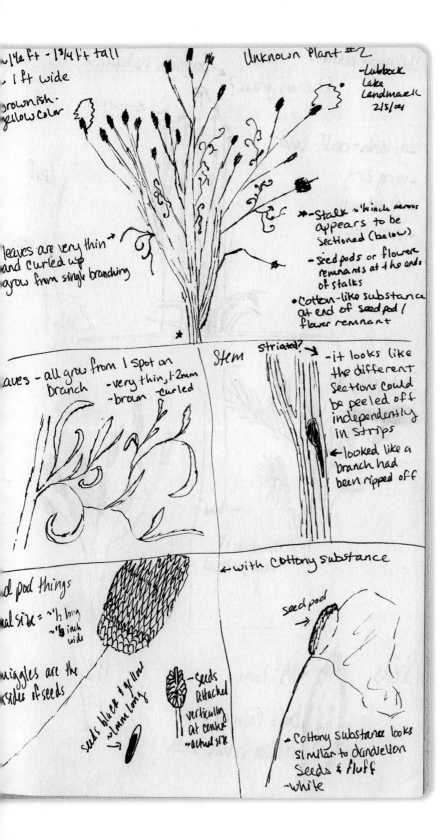

~1½ft - 1¾ft tall
~1ft wide

brownish-
yellow color

Unknown Plant #2

-Lubbock
Lake
Landmark
2/5/04

leaves are very thin →
and curled up
grow from single branching

*-Stalk ~¼ inch across
appears to be
Sectioned (below)

-seed pods or flower
remnants at the ends
of stalks

•Cotton-like substance
at end of seed pod /
flower remnant

leaves - all grow from 1 spot on
branch   -very thin, 1-2mm
          -brown -curled

Stem

striated?

-it looks like
the different
Sections Could
be peeled off
independently
in strips

←looked like a
branch had
been ripped off

←with cottony substance

seed pod things

al size = ~½ long
~⅛ inch
wide

wiggles are the
sides of seeds

seeds black & yellow
~1mm long →

-seeds
attached
vertically
at center
~actual size

seed pod
→

-Cottony substance looks
similar to dandelion
seeds & fluff
-white

Pages from Mary Porter's journal.

CORMORANT:

Twice a Cormorant was spotted. Once flying above us and another was seen swimming. But the best I could tell about their color was dark. They apeared dark brown, so maybe they were ~~Brant's~~ Cormorants. They have heavy bones, and so Double Crested the swim with their bodies mostly under water, ~~s~~treatching their necks up, and holding their beaks up. They are great divers and have webbed feet, although I never saw their feet.

A cute fact I learned from my field guide about these guys is that they stand with their wings out to dry.

you can often see them doing this

y favorite bird spotted was the COOT. I had never
een one before, or if I had, I had never noticed it.
t is roughly the size and shape of a Malard duck.
her were two swimming through the cat-tails of the
iver, and they were not very frightened by the
group of binoculars focused on them.

Red eyes
Black neck + head
Dark grey body
White tail
White bill

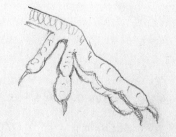

Large "lobbed" feet

Their tails remind me of cotton tailed rabbits.
The color of their legs and feet is an odd
lime green.

When they swim, their heads bob back and
forth with the stroke of their feet, like
a chicken when it walks. I never saw a
coot walk on land.

*Page from
Robert Waller's
journal.*

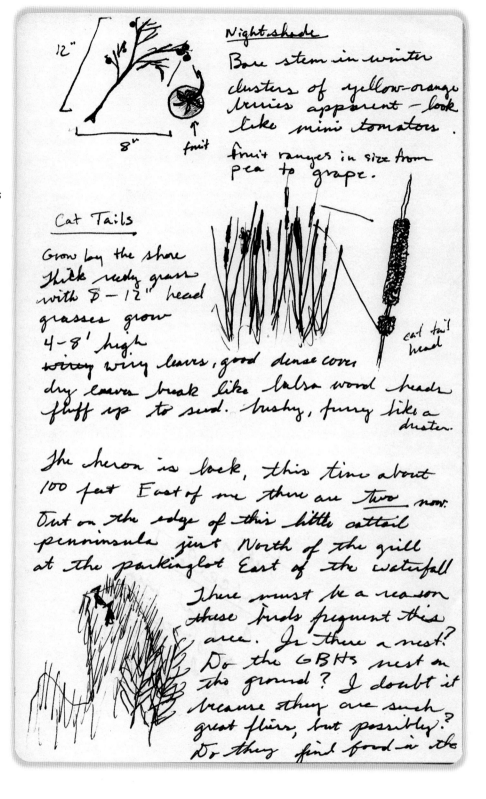

Nightshade

Bare stem in winter
clusters of yellow-orange
berries apparent — look
like mini tomatoes.

fruit ranges in size from
pea to grape.

12"

8"

↑ fruit

Cat Tails

Grow by the shore
Thick reedy grass
with 8 — 12" head
grasses grow
4 - 8' high
wiry wiry leaves, good dense cover
dry leaves break like balsa wood heads
fluff up to seed. bushy, furry like a
duster.

cat tail head

The heron is back, this time about
100 feet East of me there are two now.
Out on the edge of this little cattail
peninsula just North of the grill
at the parkinglot East of the waterfall
There must be a reason
these birds frequent this
area. Is there a nest?
Do the GBHs nest on
the ground? I doubt it
because they are such
great fliers, but possibly?
Do they find food in its

USE FRAMES

In the previous chapter on preparing the notebook, I talked about creating a cardboard template to use as a frame for your sketches. This is a trick I use fairly often—for some reason, sketching something inside a small box feels less intimidating to me than trying to draw a subject on a large, blank page. Reducing it in size and giving it boundaries (in art school, we used to call these "thumbnail sketches") breaks the project down into something that is manageable, which in turn eliminates the sense that the sketch is "serious," and thus encourages the creative process. The added bonus is that using frames neatens up a page. Text can be placed alongside the box, giving the page a storyboard effect, as seen on pages 62 and 63, from Monica Warren's notebook.

For her template, Monica used the straight edge of a plastic card; you could do this, or you could simply sketch in a rough box, as Delilah did in her journal excerpt on pages 56 and 57.

I'm like Delilah—I prefer to sketch in my frames, and I also prefer more of a square than a rectangle, as shown to the right.

You may prefer a traditional frame proportion, however, based on the so-called "golden rectangle," discussed below.

The Golden Rectangle

Artists have known for centuries that certain proportions are more aesthetically pleasing and have composed their works accordingly. Although paying attention to composition is not as critical when drawing for identification or making a daily log, on occasion you may still find it useful to do so when making your journal entries. How we arrange our images and text on the page or in our frames can be enhanced by using some simple rules of composition.

One of these rules concerns the proportions of the frame itself. It is commonly accepted that the ratio of 1:1.6, called the golden ratio or golden rectangle, is one of the more aesthetically pleasing shapes. You find the golden ratio in all sorts of places—buildings, note cards, paintings—precisely because it does appeal to our visual senses. A rough approximation of the golden rectangle is very easy to

Monica Warren used a storyboard effect to lay out these pages.

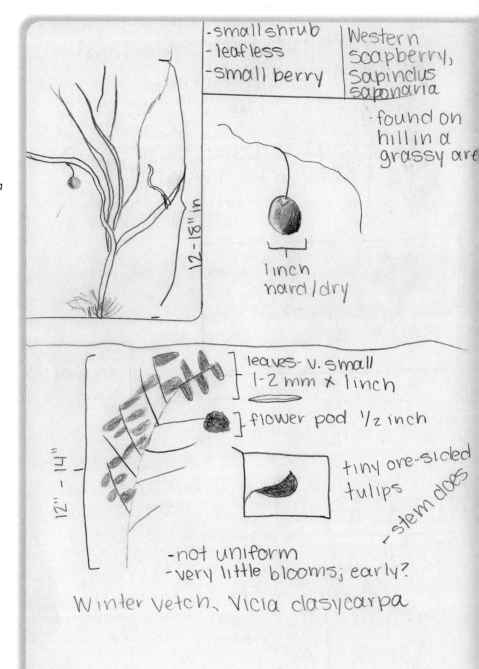

- small shrub
- leafless
- small berry

Western soapberry, *Sapindus saponaria*

- found on hill in a grassy are[a]

12-18" in

1 inch
hard/dry

leaves- v. small
1-2 mm × 1 inch

flower pod ½ inch

12" - 14"

tiny one-sided tulips

- stem does

- not uniform
- very little blooms; early?

Winter vetch, *Vicia dasycarpa*

2", spotted feet
white underneath
dark green/grey

- Great Plains Narrowmouth
- Plain Spadefoot

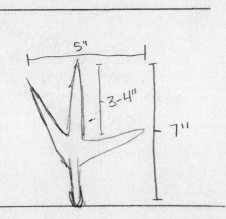

5"

3-4"

7"

Track found
in mud near a
shallow pond

- Great Blue Heron

3 toes
- long stride

draw, even without any special measuring. Simply create a square, divide it in half, and place it next to the original square, as shown here. Of course, this is not precisely 1:1.6, but it is close enough for our purposes.

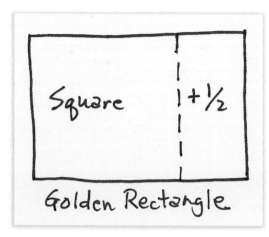

As a side note, the golden ratio is very closely related to something called the Fibonacci sequence, in which a number in the sequence is the sum of the two previous numbers. It goes something like this:

0, 1, 1, 2, 3, 5, 8, 13 . . . and so on.

As you go higher and higher in the sequence, you come ever closer to the golden ratio. And if you'll notice, if you take any two adjacent numbers, they form a rough estimate of the golden rectangle (such as 2×3, 3×5, or 5×8).

Perspective

PERSPECTIVE BASICS

Failure to draw things in perspective is a problem I see crop up over and over again in my classes. We all understand that things get smaller as they recede in the distance, but for some reason, when we sit down to sketch, we often draw only what we *know* and not what we actually *see*. For example, the illustration of the box below looks odd on the page because I have drawn it with all of its sides parallel—something that I *know* to be true.

It is also true, however, that the rules of perspective apply to all things, everywhere, even if it is so subtle it is difficult to see. Wherever you are, stop for a moment and take a look around. Everything

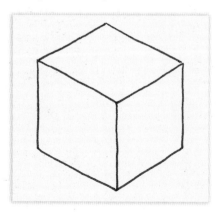

you see, unless you are looking at it straight on, converges as it recedes in the distance. The far end of a doorway is always smaller than the near end. The same is true of a table, or a sidewalk, or a forest of trees. If the object is very close to us, the effects of perspective may be minimized—this is especially true if the object is small. So a journal

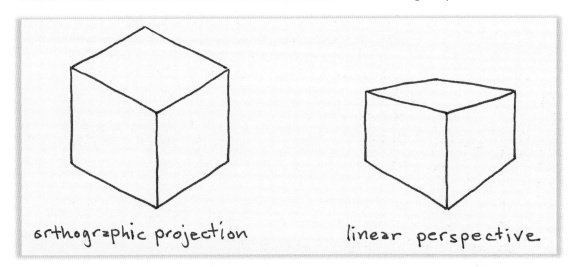

orthographic projection   linear perspective

on a table may not appear as if the far end is smaller, but it really is. If we want to draw it so that it looks realistic on the page, we may have to exaggerate the effects of perspective. Take a look at the example above, where I've drawn the box both with all the sides perfectly parallel (called orthographic projection) and with the sides slightly converging in the distance (called perspective projection).

In the first picture, the box seems as if it is tilting off the page, but in the second it appears more realistic. While you probably won't encounter many boxes in your wanderings through nature, what is true for them applies to everything else. And although it's easy to imagine how paying attention to perspective might help for the landscapes we sketch in our journals, it's less obvious how it is helpful for drawings of plants and animals. The two sketches of the box illustrate that, even on a subtle scale, attention to perspective is the difference between a subject that looks realistic on the page and one that does not, as in this journal sketch of columbine. In reality, these flowers appeared to my eyes more or less similar in size. To create a more realistic effect on the page, however, I exaggerated the perspective very slightly.

bud

fully open

shooting stars (Columbine)
Aquilegia

Fortunately, perspective is very easy to master by knowing just a few simple things. For our purposes, we need only to focus on one- and two-point perspective, which I have illustrated below.

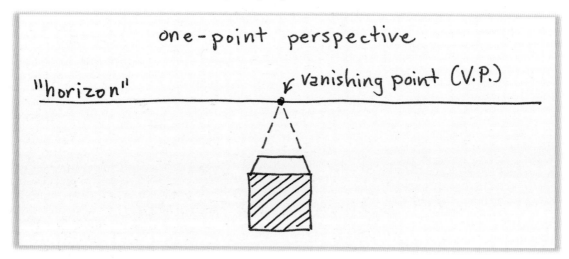

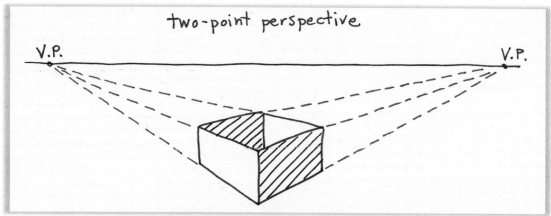

In each of these diagrams, the lines of the box converge toward what is called a "vanishing point" (V.P.) on the horizon. In one-point perspective, there is only one vanishing point, and you are looking straight on at the subject. In two-point, there are two vanishing points, and you are looking at the subject at an angle. In most cases, we use two-point perspective.

In the illustration on the previous page, the box is below eye-level—that is, you are looking down on it. The following diagrams show what a "box of trees" looks like at below and above eye-level and where the horizon line is drawn to achieve that effect.

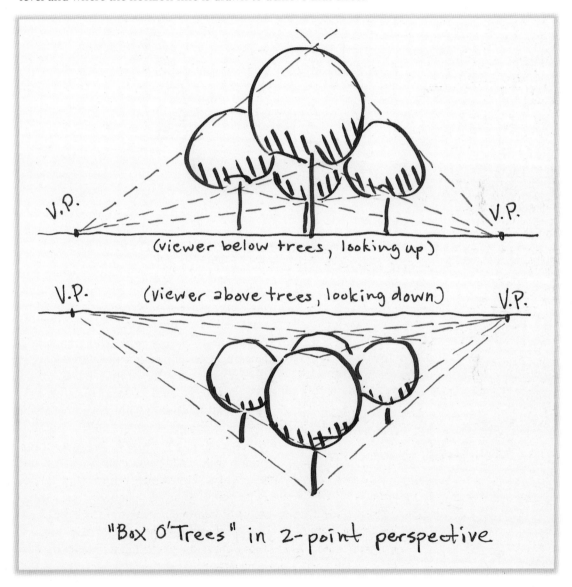

V.P.

V.P.

(viewer below trees, looking up)

V.P.   (viewer above trees, looking down)   V.P.

"Box O'Trees" in 2-point perspective

Take a look at where I've placed the vanishing points in each of the diagrams on the next page, which show what happens to the look of the box when you move the points farther out and closer in.

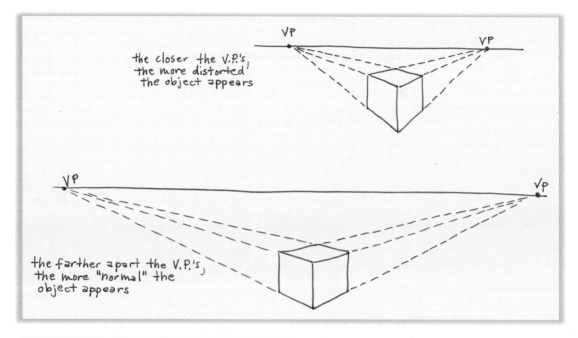

the closer the V.P.'s, the more distorted the object appears

the farther apart the V.P.'s, the more "normal" the object appears

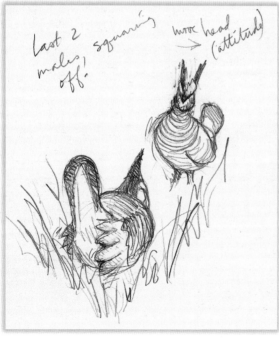

Last 2 males squaring off!

more head (attitude)

The box looks more natural when you move the vanishing points farther out, while the convergence is more exaggerated by moving them in. In the second case, the effect is the same as using a wide-angle lens on a camera. My own personal style preference is to exaggerate the effect of convergence to add dynamism to a subject, but others prefer a more realistic look. To illustrate how slight perspective exaggeration can be used to effect, here is a sketch of two male lesser prairie-chickens (*Tympanuchus pallidincinctus*) squaring off in a courtship display, shown from slightly above eye-level, in "wide-angle."

By exaggerating the perspective, I hoped to convey some of the manic energy the two birds had, even when they were still.

When you first start using perspective projection in your sketches, you will want to choose vanishing points (these will often be imaginary points that are actually off the page) and lightly draw guidelines to them. Over time and with lots of practice, you'll be able to sketch in your subject or a scene without using any guidelines at all. Here is an example from Jay Daniel's notebook that demonstrates how trees planted in a courtyard fit inside an imaginary box. Notice how each of the trees line up within the box and how the tops and bottoms of each can be traced along a guideline to show convergence toward a vanishing point.

If you need to draw objects that are evenly spaced, such as these trees in a courtyard, you can use an easy trick as shown on the next page.

Courtyard trees make an excellent subject for perspective study, and I enjoy using them precisely because it allows students to

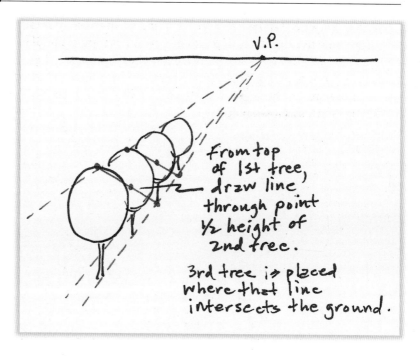

V.P.

From top of 1st tree, draw line through point ½ height of 2nd tree.

3rd tree is placed where that line intersects the ground.

become aware of how even organic subjects can fit inside a "perspective box." Later, if they are struggling to imagine how a subject might look in perspective on the page, I remind them to place it in a "box." Somewhere in your town, there are trees planted in a courtyard— seek them out and give this exercise a try.

Scenes along the Highway

SHADOWS IN PERSPECTIVE

Shadows always seem to give people trouble—they don't have to, however. The most important thing to remember about shadows is that they must lie on the same plane as the ground on which the object casting them stands, as in the example at left of juniper trees along a highway in New Mexico.

If you really want to learn how to draw cast shadows in perspective, there are all kinds of rules you can learn to get everything geometrically perfect. Since I'm usually just sketching them in my journal, however, I like to keep it as simple as possible. Here are some diagrams showing how to sketch in shadows, both when the light source is in front of and behind you.

1. The length of the shadow is determined by the placement of the "sun," as shown below:

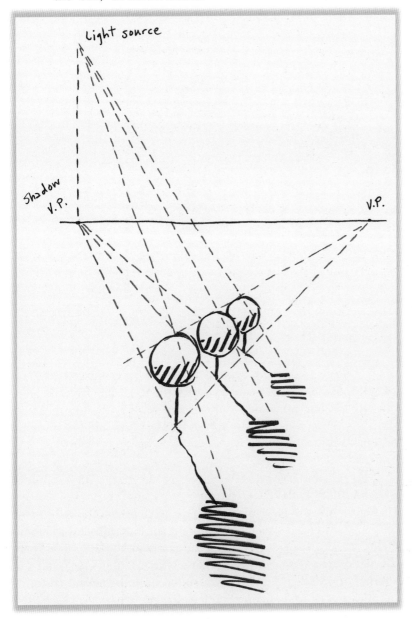

2. If the shadow is trailing away from the viewer, toward the horizon, then you create what is called a "reverse sun" to determine the length of the shadow:

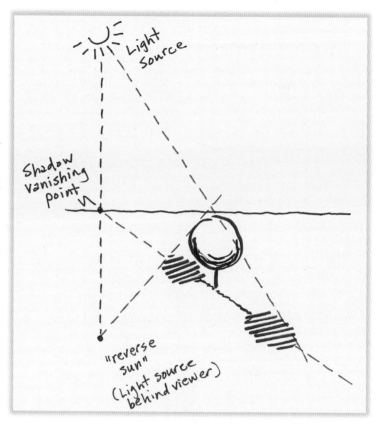

Of course, you don't usually have a shadow going two different directions in the real world—I just show it this way to show the relationship between having the sun in front of you, and the reverse, having it behind you.

AERIAL PERSPECTIVE

Finally, though you probably won't have much need for it in the context of your journal sketches, you might still find it useful to know about "aerial" perspective, which is the effect that the atmosphere has on a landscape. With aerial perspective, objects in the foreground are sharper and darker, while objects receding into the background become progressively lighter and less distinct. We have all seen this effect on mountains on the distant horizon. Not only are they progressively lighter and lighter shades of blue, but their trees, rocks, and other features disappear. Aerial perspective is easy to see in the case where there is a very distant horizon, but it is also present on a smaller scale. Take a look at a photograph of a forest or meadow and you will see that the foreground is darker and crisper than the background. Here is an example in which the trees in the background are lighter and less distinct than the shrubs in the foreground:

Hiked above Lewis & Clark's
May 31ˢᵀ campsite at   Eagle Creek
Eagle Creek. Petroglyph of.   6/1/07
h rse carved in ss. cliffs.
Ate lunch, then sat in
shade of cottonwood to sketch
the creek.
Later, we all went for a dip in
the stream. Cold, but refreshing.
                    Montana 2007

In most of the sketches you will include in your naturalist's notebook, the scale will be such that you need not concern yourself with aerial perspective. On occasion you'll probably want to sketch a landscape, and in that instance, knowing this extra little trick—making your sketch crisper and darker in the foreground—can be very useful.

These few rules for perspective should be enough to get you started. There are many other things you could learn about drawing objects in perspective projection, but I won't cover them here. If you are really interested, there are a number of fine books on the subject that you can probably find in your local library. For now, the tips I've provided in this chapter are all you'll need to know for most of the sketching you'll do in your notebook.

4. Field Drawing: Tips for the Field

I f you follow the steps I've outlined for identifying the simple shapes and building on them, and *if you practice faithfully*, you should soon be able to produce some reasonable sketches in your naturalist's journal. Even so, learning to draw out in the field presents its own challenges. Birds and other animal subjects don't sit and pose for you, trees have a dizzying number of leaves that can overwhelm you, and even wildflowers—rooted in place though they might be—have complexities that become maddening when the sun is beating down and the mosquitoes are biting. Success in the field can often

How you stand here is important. How you listen for the next things to happen. How you breathe.

—William Stafford, "Being a Person"

depend on the ability to sketch quickly, which in turn depends on the ability to edit the information you see and draw—that is, learning what elements of the subject to include and what to leave out. Here then are a few tips to help you when you are out in the field. Some of these I have already alluded to in previous chapters, and I illuminate them further here. Note, however, that these are not rules—only suggestions that might further help you visually capture the very dynamic world outside.

The first section of this chapter will address ways to learn to sketch quickly and accurately. The second section will address types of sketches that you can make.

Techniques

GET COMFORTABLE

There will be times when you are sketching very quickly and on the move. There will be other times, however, when you want to do a careful study of something. When the latter is the case, do everything you can to make yourself comfortable so that you can pay attention to the task at hand. It helps if you go into the field prepared, so here are some things I find helpful.

Take a chair or pad to sit on. If I'm going to be out in the field for a while, I like to carry along a Crazy Creek® chair. This is a kind of double cushion that sits on the ground and provides back support. It takes some getting used to, but after some practice, even this old woman finds one very easy to use—and far superior to sitting cross-legged on the ground. They are easy to strap to a pack, or if folded and carried by their handles, they make a nice tote for short distances.

If it is cold, find a place in the sun that is sheltered from the wind. If it is sunny, find some shade—and if there is no shade nearby, wear a hat. Where I live, the sun is a mighty presence, and a hat not only offers protection from the sun's heat but also shields the eyes from its harsh glare. A long day of squinting can make you tired and cranky, so a good *chapeau* can be a vital piece of equipment in your journaling toolbox. And it should go without saying that you should wear sunscreen.

I also like to carry along water or tea and a snack if I'm going to be sketching for a prolonged period of time. There's no point in being hungry and thirsty when you're trying to concentrate.

FOR MOVING TARGETS, FOCUS FIRST ON THE PARTS

The single biggest challenge to drawing birds and other animals in the field is that they don't sit and pose for you. You stare at a bird, look down to start your sketch, and look up again only to find that it has turned its head, moved its body, or flown away entirely. What to do?

Start by making a study of the parts. That is, examine the feet through your binoculars, and then make a quick sketch or two of these. Then study the bill and, again, make a couple of quick sketches. Continue doing this until you have a good feel for the individual parts of the subject. Now when you look at the bird and look away, you can concentrate on retaining an impression of the *whole* bird and fill in what you now already know of the details. Pages 78 and 79 show some examples from Jessica Meixner's journal, depicting a study on some Canada geese at a local park.

John Busby suggests this technique in his book *Drawing Birds*, where I first read about it. I, in turn, suggested it to my own students and have seen them use it with much success. Busby's book is an excellent primer on the specifics of drawings birds, and I highly recommend it if you have an interest in mastering that activity.

FOR NONMOVING TARGETS, FOCUS FIRST ON THE WHOLE

If you are sketching a nonmoving subject, such as a tree or wildflower, concentrate first on capturing the subject as a whole and then fill in details. This ensures that your proportions are right and that the underlying form is there. You may still want to make a study of the detail, but again, time is less of a factor when your subject is rooted in one place.

See pages 80–83 for more specific suggestions on drawing trees and wildflowers.

Jessica Meixner drew these geese from several different angles to capture their key features.

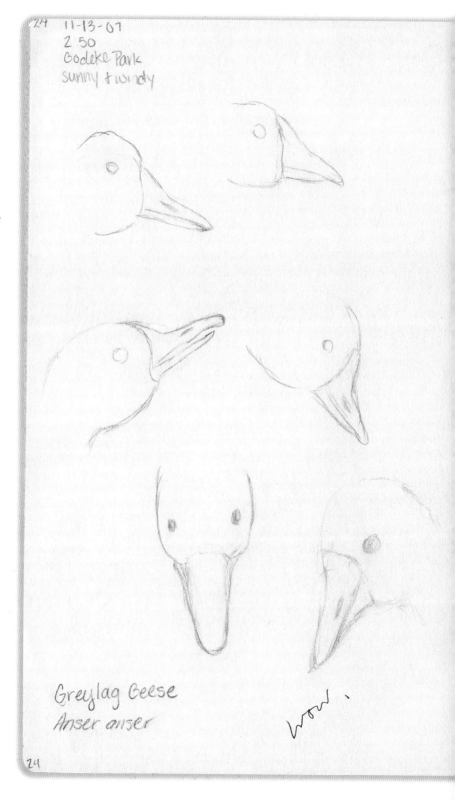

24 11-13-07
2 50
Godeke Park
sunny + windy

Greylag Geese
Anser anser

wow.

24

Wow.
terrific
study.

on ground

diving
under

kicked
back
foot

slightly
lifted
up

25

Drawing Trees and Wildflowers

Trees and wildflowers offer their own challenges even though, unlike birds, they are rooted in place and largely unmoving, thus allowing you as much time as you'd like to draw them. The difficult thing about trees and, to a lesser extent, wildflowers, is that they have an almost over-whelming profusion of detail. If it is summer, what do you do with all of those thousands of leaves? And in winter things are not much easier, because the astonishing network of branches, limbs, and twigs is revealed. It's enough to make you want to give up before you start.

The key to drawing trees is in the editing—that is, what you leave out is almost more impor-tant than what you put in. It simply isn't necessary to draw every leaf and twig, which usually clutters up the drawing and makes it impos-sible to see the *essence* of the tree.

So how do you go about edit-ing a tree sketch? The first step, as always, is to identify the overall shapes of the *whole* tree. Is the top portion—the part with the leaves and branches—conical? Cylindri-cal? Round like an apple? When I teach students to draw trees, I don't even let them put a single leaf or branch on anything until they've drawn tree shapes. To the left is an example of what I mean.

By starting this way, you learn to sketch first a rough shape of the whole tree on your page, rather than attempt to draw the tree from the tip to the base. Doing it the latter way, in fact, can cause you to run out of room on the page and almost always makes it difficult to arrive at the correct proportions.

After you begin to see the basic shapes in trees, you can start to draw a particular speci-men. Before you start, however, there are two important tips to keep in mind. They are based on how trees grow, and paying attention to them will help you create a realistic sketch.

Tree Shapes

1. **All parts of the tree narrow and divide as they go toward the terminus.** That is, the trunk narrows as it goes up and divides into smaller limbs; limbs narrow and divide into smaller branches; and branches narrow and divide into twigs. Trunks, branches, limbs, and twigs never get thicker as they grow outward and upward.

2. **The trunk is almost never more than half the height of the total tree.** In fact, it is usually less than half. The leaf canopy is how the tree gathers energy from the sun, so it comprises a significant proportion of the entire tree. Look carefully at the tree you are sketching and draw these two components in their correct proportions to one another.

Here is a quick sketch of a favorite tree in winter (i.e. without leaves) that I made one day in class to illustrate the pattern of branch growth in trees. Again, notice the way the limbs and branches narrow as they grow upward and divide to become more numerous. I've left in the faint outline of the leaf canopy that I used to start the sketch so you can picture my progress from beginning shape to finished texture.

I have not bothered to draw the branches, limbs, and twigs exactly as they appear. I suppose I could do that, but it would take a really, really long time and require much more patience than I possess.

When it comes to adding leaves, I don't bother to draw many of them, either. Rather, I try to sketch in something that is really only a rough, textured outline of the leaf canopy. I follow this with broadly shaded areas and a line texture that imitates the leaves.

If I want to show precisely what the leaf looks like (if, for example, I need to know that information for identification purposes), I make a point of drawing a single specimen to serve as an example for my notebook.

continues on next page

Drawing Trees and Wildflowers, *continued*

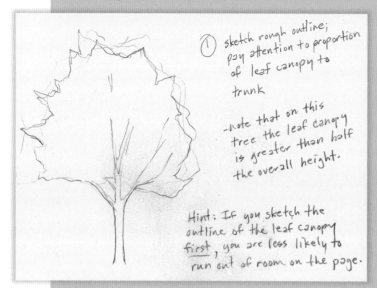

① sketch rough outline; pay attention to proportion of leaf canopy to trunk

—note that on this tree the leaf canopy is greater than half the overall height.

Hint: If you sketch the outline of the leaf canopy <u>first</u>, you are less likely to run out of room on the page.

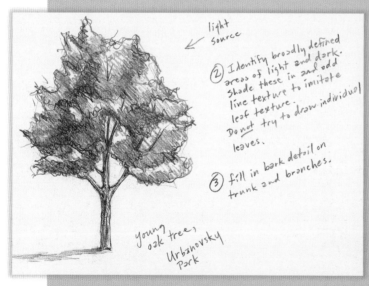

light source

② Identify broadly defined areas of light and dark. Shade these in and add line texture to imitate leaf texture. Do not try to draw individual leaves.

③ fill in bark detail on trunk and branches.

young oak tree, Urbanovsky Park

If the tree has an unusual bark, you would approach that in the same manner. Find a texture that mimics the bark for the sketch of the whole tree, and draw it in closer detail as a side note if that information is important. The point is this: we aren't trying to create photo-quality sketches for our notebooks. We are simply trying to sketch for note-taking purposes.

Wildflowers also sometimes have so many leaves and petals that they can intimidate us into giving up. There is another problem with flowers, however: they are so familiar to us that we forget to look at them. Most people have in their heads a *symbol* of a flower (most often this is a daisy), and when they sit down to draw, they have a tough time drawing anything but that. Remarkably, this is true even if the flower they are attempting to draw in no way resembles the preconceived picture in their heads. It seems that the brain wants to override what they see with what they already *know*. So with wildflowers, the real challenge is tossing out any mental history that is holding you back and really looking at what you are trying to draw.

Does it have five petals or stamens? Then you draw five, not seven or eight. The number of petals and stamens is often diagnostic (useful for identifying the flower), so if there are fewer than eight, sit there and count them and draw exactly that number. The same is true for

leaves—how many there are in a cluster or group is often important in identifying the flower.

On the other hand, if there are more than eight petals or stamens, the chances are good that the number is not diagnostic. Plus, if there are a large number of petals and stamens, you'll want to do as you do with trees and edit what you draw. That is, draw a few petals really well and sketch in the rest, as in this example of a favorite wildflower, Mexican hat (*Ratibida columnaris*).

Mexican hat is a member of the Compositae family, meaning that it actually has two types of flowers, ray and disk. The ray flowers are not usually hard to draw, but the flowers in the middle—the disks—can be difficult because they are tiny and numerous.

Mexican hat has always been a challenge for me to draw, so one morning I sat down and worked out the problem in my journal. As you can see, the purpose here was not to create a finished drawing but to understand the flower's components. It wasn't necessary to draw this complex flower perfectly; it was only necessary to draw it with enough detail that I had the information I needed. Notice that on sketch number three, I haven't tried to draw every disk flower— I have only sketched a few to hint at what they look like. And in the drawing above, I have taken care to draw a few of the individual disk flowers in close-up.

You can generally afford to include much more detail than you can with trees, and with wildflowers, you should, since any observation might turn out to be an important one.

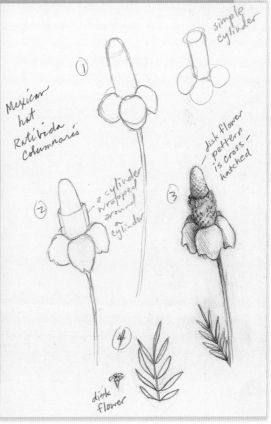

LEARN TO DOODLE

Sometimes rather than make a fully formed study, we only want to capture a quick *impression* of something—a gesture of flight, the mood evoked by trees on a hillside, or the way a road disappears into a valley. These types of sketches are notes for later use, such as for the basis of a poem, help in identifying a subject, or even later studio work. I find it useful to have some standard "doodles" in my sketching arsenal for these occasions. That is, I don't have to draw *these* trees; I only have to doodle in some trees that look roughly like them and move on. The same thing applies to any subject. In the same manner, you can do a quick doodle of a warbler gleaning a branch for insects or a stream coursing between hills. And doodles are just that—things we can practice while we're on the phone or in a boring meeting—then when you need them out in the field, they are at hand.

EXERCISES

1. Find some geese, ducks, or chickens to draw (these will be relatively easy since they tend to be more or less tame and slow-moving). Practice drawing their individual parts first, then practice drawing the whole bird.
2. Find a park or neighborhood with a wide variety of trees and practice finding their simple shapes. Take a page of your journal and fill it with the trees you find—but without drawing any leaves or branches.
3. Find a tree that seems especially attractive to you (although for the moment I'd recommend that you avoid evergreens, such as junipers, pines, cedars, and so on). Lightly sketch in the rough shape of the tree, then draw the branches as they grow, paying attention to the way they become more numerous and thinner as they grow up and outward. Also be aware of the proportion of the tree's canopy to its trunk. Don't worry about drawing leaves just yet—just try to get a feel for the form.
4. Now, on a separate page, draw the same tree with leaves. Remember that you are not trying to draw every leaf; rather, you are trying to draw an overall texture of leaves.
5. Practice exercises 3 and 4 with four more trees.
6. Find a park or neighborhood with a diversity of trees and create a page of tree doodles in your journal.
7. Locate some photos of a bird commonly found in your backyard and practice creating a "template" for it. After you have drawn two or three pages of the template birds, find the real thing and make a few pages of quick sketches. Hint: It might be easier if you keep the sketches small, both when drawing from the photos and the live birds.

I have my students practice tree doodles for their landscapes.
Here are a few examples by Jay Daniel.

PRACTICE AHEAD OF TIME

If you have practiced a particular subject—whether from photos or field guides—you will have a template in your head from which to work when you go out into the field to draw the live version. That is, you will already know how to draw what you see, so you can work

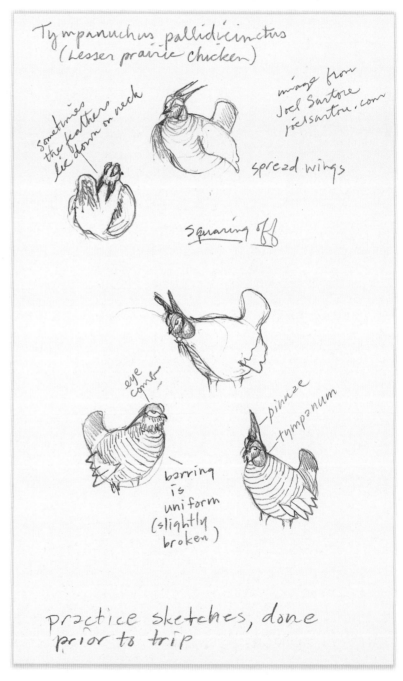

quickly and with confidence. The sketches below and to the left are from my own journal, in which I practiced drawing lesser prairie-chickens prior to making a trip to watch them booming on a lek (an open patch of ground where they do their courtship).

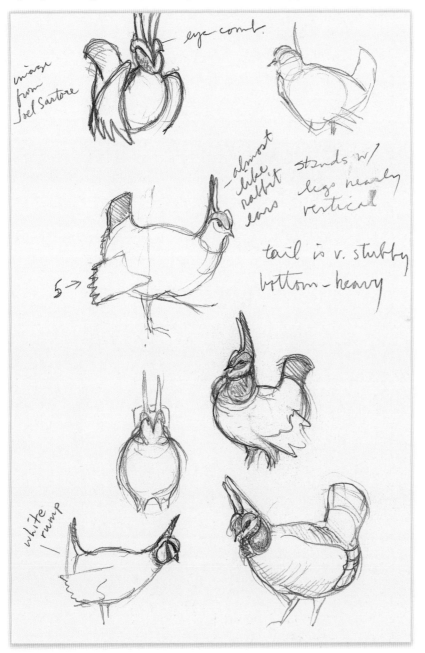

The pages below and to the right show the actual "quick" sketches done in the field. Had I not practiced first, I would have struggled to capture the live action.

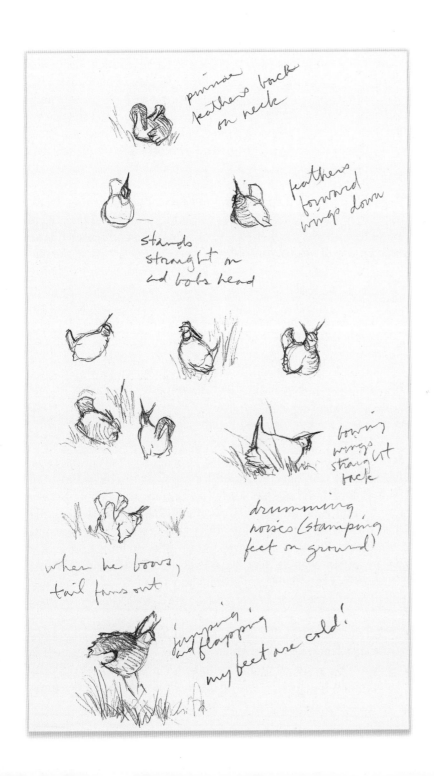

pinnae feathers back on neck

feathers forward wings down

stands straight on and bobs head

bowing wings straight back

drumming noises (stamping feet on ground)

when he bows, tail fans out

jumping and flapping my feet are cold!

Finally, recognize that the majority of your sketches are just that—*sketches*. Most of the time your work will be done quickly and look rough and incomplete. Remember that there is a dual purpose for drawing in your naturalist's journal: to heighten your powers of observation and to record information. A detail for identification, a gesture of flight or the attitude of a pose I wanted to remember for a later, more refined drawing, or a scene that struck me as unusually poignant—my own journals are filled with many small "snapshots" like these. Too much pressure to make every sketch perfect will cause your journal to be a burden instead of a pleasure. And there is a bonus hidden in here: if it is a pleasure, you will practice more, and if you practice more, your sketches will improve.

Furthermore, don't get caught up worrying about getting details just right in the field. You can always add the small stuff later. Field guides and photos can help jog your memories, and research is an excellent way to further your study of a subject.

Types of Field Sketches

There are a variety of types of sketches you will make in your notebook, but chief among them are those that you'll create for the purposes of identifying or documenting a natural subject, studies for future studio work, or sketch "notes" that you'll use to jog your memory later. Because each has a different purpose, your approach to each can be different. The following are some pointers for three different types of sketches:

SKETCHES FOR IDENTIFICATION

Sketches that you make for identification need not be beautiful or creative, but they must certainly be accurate and detailed. They should also be annotated—that is, they should include notes and labels for key features. In making these sketches, a simple, clean line drawing is often all that is necessary, as in the example on the next page by Monica Warren.

From this simple page of visual and written notes, Monica was able to later identify *Oenothera triloba*, which is also known as Texas buttercup.

As noted on pages 82 and 83, for wildflowers, you'll want to pay particular attention to the number of petals and stamens, as well as how leaves are arranged on the stem (for example, are they opposite or alternately attached?). For birds, you should be noting eye rings,

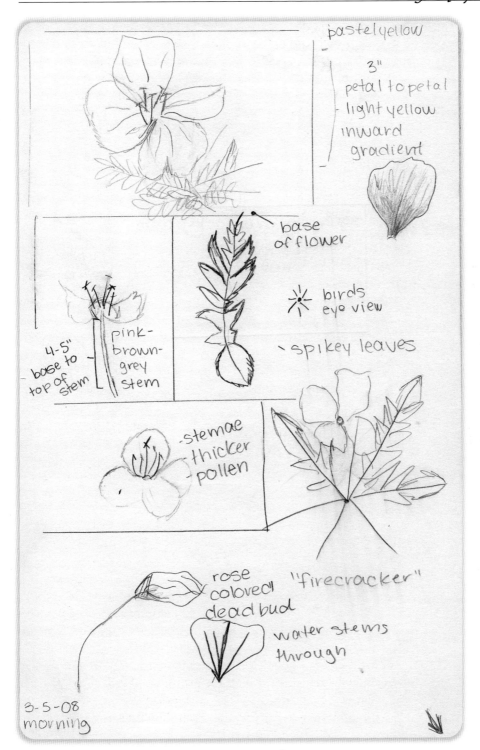

pastel yellow

3"
petal to petal
- light yellow
inward
gradient

base
of flower

birds
eye view

- spikey leaves

4-5"
base to
top of
stem

pink-
brown-
grey
stem

-stemae
thicker
- pollen

rose
colored "firecracker"
dead bud
water stems
through

3-5-08
morning

Monica Warren used clean, simple lines in these sketches for identification.

wing bars, shape of the tail (is it forked on the end?), and so on. In this kind of drawing, the same attention should be applied to all your subjects. You never know what will turn out to be important. In the example on the previous page, without even realizing its importance at the time, Monica drew the cross-shaped stigma, which is characteristic of the *Oenothera* genus.

I'll cover more information about how to look for these features (called "field marks" in birds and other animals) in the chapter on identification.

SKETCHING FOR STUDIO WORK

You may also want to include field marks and other key features when you are doing sketches for a later, more finished studio drawing or painting. For these types of sketches, however, I find it equally, if not more, important to capture the attitude or gesture of a subject and my own response to it. How did the tree look swaying in the wind? What did the hillside look like covered in wildflowers? What

about the sky with clouds scudding across it?

In sketching for studio work, you may want to make a series of small studies for the specific purpose of capturing these seemingly intangible qualities. On the following pages is a progressive series of studies I did of some cormorants while out in the field and the subsequent studio drawings that arose from it. The cormorants reminded me of something, but I couldn't quite put my finger on it until I sketched them in various poses. Eventually, it occurred to me that they looked like a famous, very moving sculpture by Auguste Rodin called *The Burghers of Calais*.

My cormorants don't do justice to that beautiful work of art, but the drawing perfectly captures for me the somber feeling I had on that day while watching them.

The first two sketches were made in the field; the second two, one of which I used to open this chapter, were created in the studio.

The Burghers of Calais I

Rawlinson 06

The Burghers of Calais II

Tomlinson 06

Your sketches for later studio work don't have to be this involved, however. Below is another example of a quick sketch I made in the field of a black-throated blue warbler. The studio drawing that arose from it is shown on the opposite page. You can see that it was little more than a snippet of information. What was important to me, however, was the attitude of his body as he clung to the tree branch.

Black throated Blue warbler

This was my first sighting of a black-throated blue warbler, a bird I'd wanted to see for years, and I thought it would be nice to commemorate the event with a drawing to hang in my office (this decision was helped by the fact that at the time I was at a workshop on bird illustration being taught by John Sill). So as I looked at him, I paid particular attention to

Black-throated blue

how he moved along that branch and committed it to short-term memory. As soon as he flew away, I pulled open my journal and made the simple sketch you see on page 94. It is shown full-size here, so you can see it wasn't a very big sketch. And, as you can also see, I didn't worry too much about the details, only about the pose. Still, in that quick little visual note, I had all I needed to get a sense of the body gesture I wanted for the final piece. I put in the sassafras leaves (a tree that was common in the region where I saw him) only after I sat down to work on the studio drawing.

SKETCHING FOR MEMORY

Sometimes when I'm in the field, I'll see something that I want to remember, but I know I don't quite have the words for it at that moment. A quick thumbnail sketch in a small frame is often sufficient to help me retain whatever it was that resonated with me. It doesn't take much—just a gesture or doodle will bring it all back for me. I find that the little thumbnail sketches sometimes serve for more than just memory aids; for me, some can be like little poems in themselves, almost like a visual haiku. To the left is an example of what I'm talking about, a quick thumbnail of something I saw on a drive home from work. It was a gloomy winter evening, and something about this large flock of blackbirds flying over the trees moved me (note the tree doodles and the frame, both of which enabled me to sketch it quickly).

5. Field Identification

From time to time we run across a bird, plant, or tree that we can't identify. There are two schools of thought about this. One is that it doesn't really matter if you don't know the names of the things around you—you can simply "be in the moment" of nature without getting all caught up in what things are called. Some might argue, in fact, that things only have names because humans have created them. After all, a bird exists as an individual regardless of whether some human comes along and says, "I shall call thee 'robin.'"[1]

Black crowned night heron

An invisible bird signs his name, bouncing his song down canyon walls

—William Wenthe, *"After Moving to a Place Where I Do Not Know the Names of Plants and Birds"*

1. The scientific name for a robin is *Turdus migratorius*—my all-time favorite name for a bird. Just saying it out loud causes me to smile every time.

The other school of thought is that knowing the names of things is very important to our experience of the natural world—not because we can use it to impress people, but because it is difficult to have a complete connection to nature without naming it. To illustrate this, think of a neighborhood. I can be "in" my neighborhood without knowing the names of the other people who live there. I can nod, smile, and wave at them when we pass on the street. We can even bake cookies for each other at Christmas or Hanukkah. But something is missing from our relationship if we don't know each other's names. When a nameless person has baked me some cookies, she's just an acquaintance, albeit a nice one. But when the cookie lady is *Nancy*, the relationship becomes one of friendship.

The analogy can be made for the natural world, too. When I hear a pleasant-sounding bird on my walk in the evening, just before dusk, I can say, "There is that pleasant-sounding bird who always sings this time of day." But when I know his name I can say, "There goes the

robin, right on time!"—and it becomes a whole new level in the relationship. You might say that without knowing the names of things you can never really be a part of the community.

Consider the poem on the following page by William Wenthe, who moved from the very green place of Virginia, where he knew the names of things, to the Llano Estacado (where I live), which was, as he once put it, like a foreign land.

Wenthe discovered that walking through a world in which he didn't know the names of things was disconcerting and unsettling. Notice that in his frustration at not knowing he even gives things pseudo-names: *breeze-twitched mustardy flowerets, dead [evergreen] grating against itself, bristle cactus twisted like antlers*. Note also the wonderful twist at the end in which the poet hears an animal that he cannot name (you sense that he is a little bit frightened because of the animal's mystery), and the terrified, nameless creature names the poet, who is in turn the terrified man—hence Wenthe's reference to this as "a kind of mirror."

After Moving to a Place Where I Do Not Know
the Names of Plants and Birds

William Wenthe

An invisible bird signs his name,
bouncing his song down canyon walls

as one might toss a pebble from the rim.

When I say the word *canyon*, shall I gather
that it holds these breeze-twitched
mustardy flowerets, or the pour
of clouds above rimrock, or shimmering
fox-color grasses on talus?

An evergreen with feathery bark,
the dead one grating against itself—
I have no name
for that, or for the birds flitting
branch to branch, their one note enough
to call each other home.

Never before such variety
of thorns: two-inch spikes on scrub branches
glisten with snagged
sunlight, bristle cactus twisted
like antlers, the ground-plant's cluster of
   green
rapiers, hooked edges
of flower-husk and leaf—

each pricking an announcement
in my skin to which I have no
reply. And none for the animal that, sensing
my approach, crackles
through underbrush, its disappearance

a kind of mirror,
a terrified name it names me.

There is a third reason as well for being able to identify things by
name: it sharpens our observations of the natural world. It is easy to
be in a place and have the sense that there is abundant life. It is easier still to know just how abundant that life is if we catalog these
things by listing the animals, plants, and insects we find. It is difficult to list them, however, if we don't know their names—witness
the lovely awkwardness of Wenthe's attempts to list things by invent-
ing long descriptors for them.

Identifying things—naming them—can be a way to deepen your
relationship with the neighborhood of the natural world both by
improving your observations of it and your connections to it. It can
also be a way to feel at ease in this world and less frightened of the
unknown. But how do you go about learning the names of things in
the neighborhood? One way is to carry field guides with you. There
are field guides for nearly anything you want to learn, including

birds, wildflowers, insects, scat, holes in the ground—the list is endless! It would be very hard indeed to carry all of these with you in your field pouch, so there are a couple of ways to approach this learning endeavor. One would be to pick only one group of animals or plants at a time, carry that guide with you until you begin to feel comfortable with your identification skills for that particular thing, then move on to another. (I did this myself for many years.) A second way to approach this problem is to use your field notebook to record the animal, insect, or plant you do not know, and then look it up when you get home (this is assuming that you have collected a library of field guides—however, if this is not the case, you can always go to a public library to do your research). This chapter will teach both how to use guides in the field, as well as how to take the right notes for identification when you don't have one with you.

Taxonomic Classification

While common names are easy and fun to use (who doesn't like saying "hog potato"?), they can often be confusing. For example, the wildflower "Ozark sundrop" is also known as just plain "sundrops," as well as "Missouri primrose," "fluttermill," and "yellow evening primrose." You and I might know it by different names, and that could get in the way of communicating information. And that's not all—sometimes the same common name is used for different genera or species, as is the case with *Calylophus berlandieri*, another member of the primrose family whose common name is "sundrops." With most organisms we encounter in our outside perambulations, particularly wildflowers, it is very useful—even recommended—to learn the scientific name as well as the common. That way, when we say *Oenothera missouriensis*, we can be sure we are talking about the same thing. Furthermore, while "yellow evening primrose" might tell me we are talking about a flower in the primrose family, "sundrop" does not. *Oenothera*, however, is the name of the genus to which many of the flowers commonly called primroses belong, and we also know that *missouriensis* tells us where this species was first found and named by a taxonomist.

Often the origins of scientific names give us interesting, if baffling, clues about the natural history of the organism. For example, the evening primroses belonging to the genus *Oenothera* get their scientific names from the Greek root of *Onos* (ass) and *thera* (to chase or pursue). Why this relatively harmless-looking plant would be pursuing a donkey is beyond me . . .

Onos is also the basis of the family name, Onagraceae, whose ending, "aceae," means "belonging to."

That being said, this down-home girl still likes to call things by their common, or folk, names—names that were given not because there was a need for taxonomic classification but because the plants, birds, or whatever were woven into the fabric of the namer's everyday life, and the names carry some of the meaning they had to that person. Retaining and using the common name connects me to a folk tradition and lends further richness to my relationship with the organism I'm studying. If there is a chance I'll be misunderstood, I'll then follow with the scientific name.

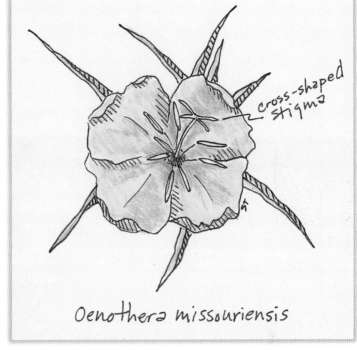

Oenothera missouriensis

THE SYSTEM OF TAXONOMIC CLASSIFICATION

A few notes on the order of taxonomic classification might be helpful here. The Linnaean system of classification (the most universally used) groups organisms into a hierarchy, beginning with Kingdom and ending at the species level. The system (in its simplest form here) looks like this:

Kingdom
     Phylum (animals) Division (plants)
       Class
         Order
          Family
           Genus
            Species

In this system, the Kingdom is divided into phyla, which are in turn divided into classes, and so on all the way down. A *family* is a large group of morphologically similar *genera*, which in turn are groupings of *species* that share even more specific traits. Family names are never italicized, but generic and specific names always are. Generic names are also always capitalized. So it is written in this way:

Family

Genus

species

In most instances, you will deal primarily with families and below, and all organisms are usually referred to using their *binomial nomenclature*—their genus and species names.

PRONUNCIATION OF SCIENTIFIC NAMES

Since I find it difficult to learn things I can't pronounce (how can you memorize a word if you can't repeat it in your head?), one of the more useful things my ornithology teacher ever did for me was to give some general guidelines on how to pronounce scientific names. I'd like to do the same for you, so here are a few tips to get you started[2]:

- Always pronounce the last vowel.
- *ae* or *oe* are usually pronounced as a long *e* ("ee").
- When *ae* is preceded by a vowel, pronounce the first as a long vowel, and follow it by the "ee" sound.
- Words of more than two syllables are stressed on the second to last syllable if the vowel in the syllable is long, or if it is followed by two consonants; otherwise, it is stressed on the third to last syllable.

So using the rules above, we would pronounce *Oenothera* as "ee-no-THEE-ra," and *Onagraceae* as "oh-nah-GRAH-see-ee." Here are few more helpful rules:

- When *i* is added to a commemorative name, as in *wilsoni* (after Alexander Wilson, an eighteenth-century naturalist often credited with being the father of American ornithology), pronounce it as "eye."
- When there is a double *i* (*ii*), it is pronounced "ee-eye."

2. These are from "Pronunciation of Biological Latin: Including Taxonomic Names of Plants and Animals." http://www.saltspring.com/capewest/pron.htm. Many other helpful tips and examples can be found there as well.

So *Thryomanes bewickii*, a little wren named for Thomas Bewick, a friend of John James Audubon and a fellow illustrator, is pronounced: *"thry-OH-mah-nees bew-ICK-ee-eye."*

There are more rules for pronouncing scientific Latin (and of course, exceptions to the rules I've outlined above), but I find that these get me by with most names I run into. Furthermore, once you've learned a few scientific names, it becomes easier to figure out new ones intuitively.

Some people claim that there are no rules to pronouncing scientific names, but I find that notion unsettling and one that would surely lead to chaos. Even if you don't use these particular rules, you will probably be more comfortable if you at least make up some general rules of your own.

METHODS OF IDENTIFICATION

Some field guides group organisms according to color; yellow flowers are together in one section, orange birds in another, and so forth. While at first glance this seems user-friendly, it is not an ideal way for the serious naturalist to go about identifying things. For one thing, some colors are very common—the number of yellow wildflowers is simply staggering. Lumping them all together does next to nothing for narrowing down your choices in order to make your identification easier. Furthermore, one person's idea of blue might be someone else's idea of green. Or what looks green in some light might look brown in another. On the whole, while color can be an important diagnostic feature, it is not a useful way to start the identification process.

Lesquerella gordonii "bladder pod" ~ ¼"

More importantly, though, an organism is more than just its name. A plant or animal is classified into family, genus, and species because it is related to others in those groupings. Locating something in a field guide through color may be possible, but it doesn't help us know that the eastern bluebird and the American robin are both members of the thrush family (Turdidae), since in a color-coded field guide, one would be found with birds that are blue and the other with birds that are red. Knowing that a bird is a thrush, on the other hand, tells us something about its behaviors and habitat; the life history of a thrush is not the same as that of a blue jay or a cardinal—birds that are also known for their blue and red colors.

I really can't stress this last point enough. It is much more useful and informative to know that the yellow flower you've just identified as bladderpod is in the mustard family than it is to simply know what it is called. Mustards are easily identified by their four petals and six stamens (four tall, two short). Their former scientific name, Cruciferae (they are now called Brassicaceae), even reflects this, as their petals do indeed form a cross. Mustards are extremely handy plants to have around, as they have long been valued for both their culinary and medicinal uses. Mustards such as broccoli, cauliflower, turnips, rutabaga, and so on, are commonly found on our dinner tables. And for many years, members of this family were used routinely to treat colds and congestion—you can often find references to mustard poultices in novels written many years ago. You can still harvest some wild mustards to use as herbs or food, but first you'd need to know what to look for (not all are edible or palatable).

A general hint on the matter of identifying plants or animals

There are countless different species of organisms in the world. Narrowing down the possibilities would be a maddening task if it were not for one lucky fact: only a few of them occur in any geographic location at a time. Whether you are traveling or exploring your home ground, try to obtain checklists specific to the region. By referring to the checklist, you can quickly determine what is likely to be found in the area, which will make your identification task much easier.

If you were to leaf through your field guide searching for a yellow flower among the hundreds of possible candidates, you might never find it. But if you know that it's a mustard, you can still come away from the field with some knowledge about it in a general way (because you have studied the family), even if you didn't have the opportunity to put a name to that particular little cross-shaped yellow flower you saw.

The best way to start the identification process is to learn the key characters necessary for identifying the organisms in which you are interested. This will allow you to separate them into families, then genera, and finally species. While I can't teach you about all the organisms you might encounter in the field, I can teach you a little of the processes for identifying wildflowers and birds. From these two slightly different approaches, you can extrapolate the means to identify almost anything in nature. Then, if you take a particular interest in lizards, or mice, or beetles, you can use some of the same tricks to identify them.

FOR YOUR NOTEBOOK

A couple charts on wildflowers that you can photocopy and place in your field notebook can be found on pages 117 and 118. You can either glue them directly on the frontispiece of your journal, or do as I do and laminate them and place them in a pocket you've glued there.

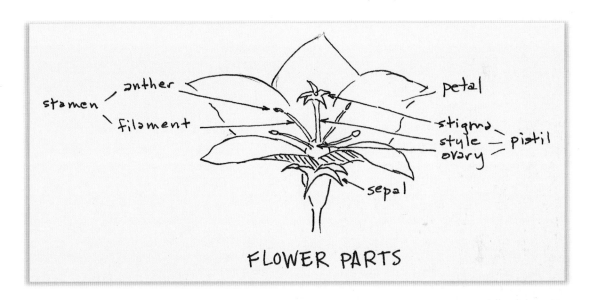

FLOWER PARTS

Wildflowers

We'll start with wildflowers, since they are easiest to identify by first "keying"[3] them into families. After that, it's relatively easy to locate the possibilities of genera and species in the field guide. And once you've learned these families, if you run across a flower that doesn't seem to fit into one of them, you'll not only know what sort of key characters to make note of in your journal, you'll also have narrowed the possibilities of other families to which it might belong. I've provided a diagram of the key parts of flowers above. Your field guide should have one of these, too, as well as examples of leaf patterns. At the end of this chapter, you'll find a list of some of the more common families, along with a short descriptor and diagrammatic drawing of a representative flower or plant part.

3. The true process of "keying out" is actually more involved than this, but it isn't something we need to use here.

IN THE FIELD: *Identifying Wildflowers*

You are walking along a trail you've traveled many times before. Suddenly, you notice a plant that has always been there, but is so relatively unremarkable that it escaped notice until today. It is only six or eight inches tall, and there are numerous miniscule, delicate, gray-green leaves. They are distinct in that they have "leaflets" that are slender and narrow and arranged like miniature soldiers all in a row. And there are clusters of tiny flowers as well—so tiny that they are hard to see unless you peer closely. When you do lean in for a better look, you find that the flowers have five striking, yellow-ochre petals that are irregularly arranged (bilaterally symmetrical), with ten reddish-brown stamens clustered in the center, as if they are standing at attention. The flowers are growing in a cluster along a stalk (called a raceme) that sticks up from the top of the plant.

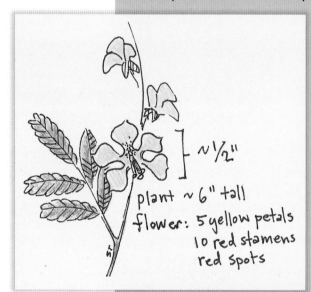

plant ~ 6" tall
flower: 5 yellow petals
10 red stamens
red spots

~ ½"

At this point, you can pull out your handy wildflower family chart from your journal and you'll find that the leaves alone help you place this in the legume family, Fabacae (Leguminosae is the former name).

You sketch the leaf and the flowers for identification. Besides allowing you to slow down and really examine the plant, this will be useful for reference if you haven't brought a field guide with you. The sketch can be simple, and it might look something like the one shown here.

If you have brought a field guide with you, that's terrific. Hopefully it is a regional field guide, because confining the list of wildflowers to just those found in the area will help greatly to narrow the possibilities.

When you do have your guide in front of you, you can turn to the legume family's photos, and you'll find a picture of a flower called hog potato, or *Hoffmanseggia glauca*. It looks like a good match (it's a pretty distinctive flower), but to be sure you turn to the text for confirmation. There you find that the diminutive size of the plant alone narrows the possibilities down to this one choice in the region. If there had been other photos of other legume flowers that looked similar, this last step would have helped tremendously in parsing the differences.

FAMILIES

Once you've figured out to which family your wildflower belongs, you can turn to that section in your guide and match it to a photo-graph. It is usually easy to spot which one it is, but in some cases, there might be several species that look very similar. If that is the case, you will need to read the descrip-tion that is associated with each photo for further clues to which flower yours might be. *Do not skip this last step!*—many flowers are dis-tinguishable from their colleagues only by some minute detail that you might otherwise miss. One example is that of blackfoot daisy (*Melam-podium lucanthum*) and lazy daisy (*Aphanostephus ridellii*). Found in the unwieldy Compositae family, they appear to be very similar both in

gray streaks on underside

Melampodium leucanthum

photos and real life to someone unfamiliar with them. Blackfoot daisy, however, has fine, dark gray streaks on the underside of its petals—and though these can be used to positively identify the flower, this is not something you'd know by looking at a photo. To

Should you collect wildflowers for study?

The answer is yes and no. Some species are very abundant, while others are not. Certainly in the latter case, there is danger that you could be putting pressure on that species' chance of survival.

Here are a few rules most people use for collecting:

1. Never do it in a city, state, or national park (it is illegal).
2. If the flower is on private property, never do it without the owner's permission.
3. Never do it if there are fewer than ten plants in the immediate area.
4. And never, ever do it if you know the plant to be a protected species (this is also illegal).

My own feeling is that the best practice is simply to use your sketchbook or a camera.

As a side note, there are some groups of people who will perform "plant rescues" if an area is being destroyed by construction. In these instances, they collect the plant and transplant it to another suitable location. If you are interested in this practice, you might check with your local garden club or Audubon society to see if there is someone doing that in your area.

illustrate how important this tiny detail is, even though I'm very familiar with *Melampodium* (I grow it in my garden), there are some days in the field that it looks very much like *Aphanostephus*, even to me, so I always use this detail to assure myself that I'm looking at this species. And again, without reading the description in the guide, I wouldn't know about it.

Birds

*M*y approach to identifying birds is very different from the technique I use for wildflowers. For one thing, birds are not rooted to the ground, waiting patiently as I count the number of feathers in their tails. They don't generally like it when you try to get close enough to see them with the naked eye, and even when you're looking at them through binoculars, they move around a lot—some of them very quickly. They also have a frustrating tendency to disap-

pear among the leaves of a tree just when you think you are about to get a good look at them. What this often boils down to is a very short time in which to examine your subject. You usually do not have the luxury of leafing through a field guide, page by page, looking for a bird that you do not know. This means you will be served by knowing something about what birds you might see before going out into the field.

A word on how most field guides are arranged

It may appear that there is no clear pattern to the listings in guides and checklists, but there is an organization method. The arrangement is based on taxonomic order—that is, position on the list is determined by scientists' best understanding of the evolutionary history of birds, with the oldest order appearing first and the most recent order last. Though there are different versions of taxonomic order, most North American guides and checklists follow the one created by the American Ornithologists' Union (AOU).

It is really much easier for most of us to separate birds into their respective families than it is for wildflowers, since most of us already do so without thinking about it. Everyone knows what a duck looks like, for example, and that it is markedly different from a sparrow or a hummingbird, each of which belong to their own families. Using what we already know as our foundation, it is simply a matter of learning what the different families are and filling in the details.

One of the best ways to get familiar with the bird families is to study your field guide on a regular basis. Sit down with it after dinner when the dishes are done, take it along on a picnic, or cozy up with it in front of a fire on a winter evening. Thumb through the guide, paying attention to what the different families are, what the birds in those families look like, and where they are located in the guide (most guides will have them listed in an order that starts, very roughly, with birds you will find on or near the water, proceeding through birds of prey, followed by small "dickey" birds, and finishing up with the sparrows). Over a remarkably short time, you'll have a good sense of what family a bird belongs to, and from there the going gets a lot easier. I can't emphasize enough that studying the guide beforehand to become familiar with the different families is important for one very good reason: birds don't sit still for a detailed keying out the way that wildflowers do! If you have a good sense of what to be on the lookout for before you go out, you will be much more successful at your endeavor.

When you do go out to the field and spot something you want to identify, take the time to examine the bird as carefully as possible before it flies away. Study the bill, head shape, color of the legs, and so on. When you feel you have a good mental picture, you can pull out the guide and start looking at the possibilities. If you don't already know to what family it belongs, think about where you saw the bird: Was it on the water? Look toward the front of the guide for answers. On the shore? Look a bit farther in, more toward the middle, where you will find shorebirds. Was it perched on a telephone wire? Well then, it's a good bet that it's going to be somewhere in the vast order of Passeriformes, or perching birds, which are found in the second half of the book.

One helpful trick you might try to locate bird groups quickly in your guide is to index the side. Some newer field guides have started using integrated indexes, but you can make your own if yours doesn't have this feature. I got this idea many years ago from a magazine article I read. Sadly, I can't remember which magazine, or who the author was, as I'd like to give credit where it is due; in any case, it is a very useful field trick indeed. I divide the book into the following categories: *ducks, hawks, grouse, rails, sandpipers, gulls, alcids, owls, hummers, flycatchers, vireos, swallows, thrushes, warblers, sparrows,* and *blackbirds.* I turn to the section where each group starts (e.g., I open the book to the "woodpecker" section) and mark a line from that page to the edge of the book with a medium red felt-tipped pen. Then I write the name of the group to the side of/above that in a

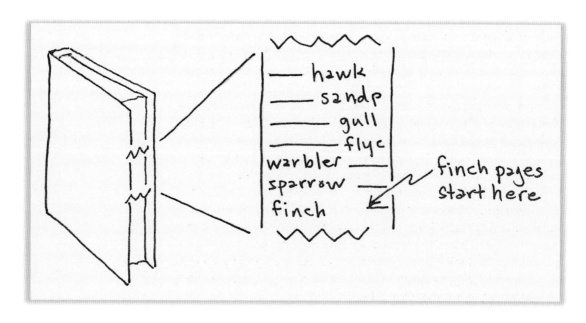

About Technique

Birds can be very sensitive to movement—perhaps more so than to sound. I find I can talk in a conversational tone with a friend while standing near a flock of birds without raising any alarms. If I make any sort of sudden movement, however, no matter how small, they will fly away. (This is one reason blinds are so useful for drawing and photographing birds.) So move slowly and deliberately, and try not to wave your arms around too much.

In fact, sometimes the very best way to see a lot of birds is to go to a place where you know them to be, find a comfortable place to sit, and then settle in and wait. After a while, they'll feel comfortable enough to return, and you can then observe to your heart's content. Patience is a valuable tool in field work.

On the same note, birds don't generally seem to care what color someone's clothing is (and they probably aren't fooled by camo), although some birders think that it helps to wear a hat. Birds that are normally prey are probably watching your eyes to determine whether you are a threat, and a hat helps to hide these.

Finally, if you spot a bird in the distance and you suspect it's one you really want to see, pause to take a good look at it through your binoculars before rushing over to it. In fact, pause every few feet and take more looks. That way, if the bird decides to up and fly away before you get close enough for a *really* good look, you've at least seen something—maybe even enough to make a positive identification.

finer-tipped pen, so that the edge of the book looks more or less like the illustration on the previous page.

This is just a small sample of what the indexed side looks like, of course—in the real thing, all the categories I've listed would be written there. The line to the side of each group of birds marks where those pages begin.

This system has served me well for many years. When I want to *quick—look up that swallow!*—I can open to that section immediately. This is not a comprehensive index, but it covers the most common groups I run across in the field. Any more than these, and I find the side of the book becomes cluttered and hard for me to read.

You might think of another way to index the guide—I encourage you to experiment with it. After all, it's another way to become familiar with both the guide and the birds within. One thing I will mention, however: I have tried indexing the side using both paper and plastic tabs that stick out and have been less than happy with this arrangement. They just seem to catch on things and annoy me. But you should try it if it sounds good to you.

FIELD MARKS

Once you have figured out to what family your bird belongs, you'll want to pick out the key field marks that will help you determine that your bird is one species, and not another very similar one. Sometimes this is easy; for example, though they belong to the same family, an American robin looks nothing like a hermit thrush. For other species it can be much more difficult, and this is where the key field marks become crucial. It helps to be familiar with the feather topography—the patterns made by the different feather groups—since many of these make good field marks. Most field guides have very nice diagrams of these patterns, and it is useful to study them. That way, when your guide refers to them in a description or an illustration, you will know what is meant. And once you've narrowed the possibilities down to two or three species, a check of these descriptions or diagrams will let you know which field marks are characteristic of a particular species.

Many field marks are actually different feather groupings, so it's useful to learn these; one of the best ways I know to learn them is to draw and label a bird. Find two or three photos of a bird you like, open your field guide to the pages diagramming the topography, and set to work. In my example on the next page, I've chosen the oven bird, simply because I like its tidy, handsome head and breast. The oven bird is by no means a perfect model, however. Aside from the head and breast, its overall coloring is rather uniform (I've exaggerated it here to emphasize the feather groupings). For your first bird, you might look for one with more distinctive feather markings. Also, many birds don't have an eye ring or crown stripe like the oven bird, or they might have an "eyebrow" and wing bars, which are features this bird lacks. The bird you choose to draw may or may not have these, too.

Identifying Field Marks

There are certain key field marks I routinely make note of any time I'm looking at birds. Here is a list of what I look for:

- presence/absence of eye ring
- presence/absence of wing bars
- shape and size of bill
- color of legs
- color of rump, undertail coverts, breast
- head markings, such as malars, "eyebrows" (supercilium), and crown stripes
- breast/neck markings, such as "stick pins" and "collars"

In time, you will develop a sense of what is an important field mark. When you find a bird you've never seen before, you will mentally tick these off so that when you look in your guide, you will be more likely to positively identify it.

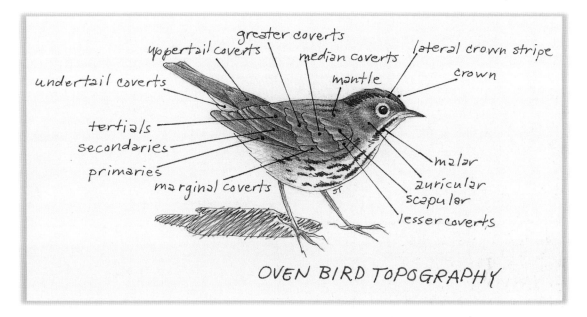

greater coverts
uppertail coverts
median coverts
lateral crown stripe
undertail coverts
mantle
crown
tertials
secondaries
primaries
marginal coverts
malar
auricular
scapular
lesser coverts

OVEN BIRD TOPOGRAPHY

BEHAVIORS

Behaviors are often as important as field marks in helping us with birds that are especially hard to identify. Little things, such as whether the head is bobbing or the tail is cocked at a particular angle, can give us important clues. For example, every year around the first of March, I take a canoe trip down a river in Texas. While there, when I see a medium-sized sandpiper standing on the banks, bobbing its whole body up and down, I know that it's the spotted sandpiper, even though *there isn't a single spot to be found*. At this time of year, the spotted sandpiper is still in winter plumage, and thus this bird used to fool me each year until I finally learned to look first for the bobbing motion rather than rely on field marks.

ENVIRONMENT/HABITAT

The habitat in which you find your bird can also be a useful and important bit of information when you are trying to identify a bird (or, for that matter, any organism). You wouldn't expect to find a grassland bird in a forest or a shorebird in the desert. This may seem obvious, but for many birds it isn't immediately apparent what their natural habitat is. For example, you might assume that all sparrows are the same in what they prefer for their living environment, but

IN THE FIELD: Identifying Birds

You spy a small bird flitting around in a tree. You notice that the bird is very active, searching for only a couple of inches along one branch for food and then jumping to another. In fact, this bird seems to be in constant motion.

- Approach the tree by walking swiftly and quietly until you are within a few feet of it, then slow your movements down—the bird might be skittish about your presence.
- Stand quietly for a few moments and locate the bird using just your eyes.
- Once you have located the bird with your eyes, quickly and smoothly raise the bins without moving your head. At this point, the bird may or may not be in your binoculars' field of view—this is really a zippy little bird that doesn't stay in one spot for very long, so it may take two or three tries to get a good look.

Now that you have the bird in your sights, you notice a few obvious field marks:

- the overall color of the bird is a grayish brown, but there might be a hint of greenish yellow
- the body of the bird is "stubby" looking (as opposed to slender)
- there is a distinct broken eye ring
- there are two whitish wing bars on each wing (these are formed by the variation of color—in this case white—on the bottom edge of the median and greater coverts)
- the bill is short, thin, and black

If this is a bird that is completely unfamiliar to you, other field marks worth noting might be:

- any other head markings (in this case, they are absent on our mystery bird)
- color of the legs (black)
- angle of the tail (on the same plane as the back; that is, not "cocked" or "droopy")
- whether the wings are folded above or below the tail, or flat against the rump (folded above)

You watch the bird carefully for a few more minutes, making as many mental notes as you can, when it suddenly flies away. Now you can decide to give chase, or you can stop and make notes (and perhaps a quick sketch) in your notebook.

Possibilities based on field marks, environment, and behavior:

    warbler sp.*

    kinglet sp.

    empidonax sp.

    wren sp.

    vireo sp. (though these are not quite as frenetic in their behavior)

If you are a beginning birder, you might not know that these are even the possibilities—even so, you know more than you think. For example, you know it isn't a duck, owl, hawk, sparrow, or hummingbird. This is where practice and experience come into play, for after you have spent even just a little time at this business of identification, you'll find that you'll begin to develop a feel for what it *isn't*, and that narrows the choices considerably.

When you look up your mystery bird in your field guide, you check your notes (mental and otherwise) against the possibilities in the list above. The bird is stubbier than a vireo, warbler, or "empid," and more gray than a wren and without the characteristic "barred" pattern of that family. So in the end you determine that the mystery bird is a ruby-crowned kinglet.

But wait! You didn't actually see the "ruby crown," which is clearly depicted in the illustration. Many birds have special colored feathers, called "badges," that are often hidden. Under certain circumstances, however, they will flash these badges, possibly to establish social status; these are therefore depicted in the field guides. So just because you didn't see this particular field mark, don't rule out the kinglet. All the other field marks clearly point to this bird. Plus, if you read the description in the guide carefully, you'll probably find that it mentions that the ruby crown is seldom seen.

---

*When we know what genus something is, but aren't sure about the species (which we don't know at this point), we refer to the generic group, followed by the word "species." In our notation, we usually write this as "sp."

this isn't so. A grasshopper sparrow will only be found in the grasses of the plains, while a seaside sparrow is found in the salt marsh grasses of the coast. Exactly where the bird is located in the habitat is just as important. A junco is a ground feeder, so look for it to be scratching around there for food. The same is true of the spotted towhee, which you can expect to find kicking up dead leaves. On the other hand, you will probably not find many warblers on the ground. In fact, though most warblers can be found in trees, some prefer the lower parts of trees, while you might expect to see others near the tops.

When you spot a bird, pay attention to these details—in addition to teaching you something about the bird's life history, they could help you figure out what it was you saw.

That's it—that's all you need to know to get started identifying things. Now you need only practice in order to become proficient at it. As you improve, you may want to take on more advanced tasks such as identifying birds by sound or using a microscope to identify the many kinds of algae.

Bird "Jizz"

Behaviors and habits also help us when we need to rely on the "jizz" of the bird to make our call. Jizz is a slang term used by birders stemming from an acronym for "general impression of shape and size," or "GISS." Sometimes we can't get a good look at a bird (a hawk flying far in the distance, for example), or maybe we've only seen it for the briefest moment before losing it again. If we are in luck, something about the bird will look familiar—perhaps the way it cocked a tail, or how short and stubby the wings looked compared to the rest of the body. Behaviors are something that can add to a bird's overall jizz, so that we can say, "There's a spotted sandpiper!" even as the current carries our canoe downstream faster than we can get our bins out for a good look. After all, it is the right range, right habitat, right size, right shape, and there's that funny bobbing motion. In this instance, no field marks are needed.

Or sometimes jizz can alert us that we are *not* looking at what we expect. There's just something a little off about the way that sparrow is acting. You decide to take a closer look, and the next thing you know, you've spotted a rarity from Mexico.

It is important to remember that jizz is an impression—and that means we could be wrong from time to time. It is always better to get a good look at the bird when possible before making an identification.

But whatever route you choose to take, once you begin to name the things in your neighborhood, you also begin to deepen your relationship with the natural world.

Common Wildflower Families

Photocopy this chart and the one on the next page and paste them in your journal. Or make a two-sided copy and laminate it to make a card.

COMMON WILDFLOWER FAMILIES

(Information adapted from *Wildflowers of the Western Plains* by Zoe Merriman Kirkpatrick)

	CACTACEAE	(Cactus Family)	Succulent, with spines
	ASTERACEAE (Compositae)	(Daisy, Sunflower, or Aster Family)	Appears to be one flower, but is actually composed of outer ray flowers and inner disk flowers
	BRASSICACEAE (Cruciferae)	(Mustard Family)	Four petals, usually small, arranged in a symmetrical "cross"
	GERANACEAE	(Geranium Family)	Radially symmetrical flowers with five fused petals; long "beaklike" fruit ("stork's bill")
	LAMIACEAE (Labiateae)	(Mint Family)	Bilaterally symmetrical, square stems, opposite leaves; mint smell

COMMON WILDFLOWER FAMILIES *continued*

	FABACEAE (Leguminosae)	(Bean or Legume Family)	Compound, pinnate leaves
	MALVACEAE	(Mallow Family)	Symmetrical flowers with five petals and many fused stamens
	ONAGRACEAE	(Evening Primrose Family)	Symmetrical flowers, with four petals and four sepals; usually eight stamens; flowers are tubular at base
	SCROPHULARIACEAE	(Snapdragon Family)	Bilaterally symmetrical; five fused petals (two upper and three lower)
	SOLANACEAE	(Potato or Nightshade Family)	Symmetrical flowers; five fused petals
	VERBENACEAE	(Vervain Family)	Five petals, slightly irregularly arranged; square stems and opposite leaves

6. Putting It All Together

Now you know how to do a little sketching and use guides to identify plants and animals you find in the field. You have some of the basic tools to start—all that remains is to add your notes. But what sort of notes should you be making? And in what format? Well, that depends on what it is you want to do with your notebook.

Sometimes I go out to the field to collect data for scientific research, sometimes to sketch a pleasant scene, write a poem, or just get my Zen back. And sometimes I do a combination of all these things, and I have to focus my attention and heighten my senses so that I can record as much detail in the field as possible. Doing so enables me to return to my studio and recreate what I saw, smelled, and heard. I can also research plants or animals, or whatever else caught my attention when I was there, using my notes as a starting point on the page and filling in any new details

If your father was a redbird
Then you would be obligated to try to understand
What it is you recognize in the sun
As you study it again this evening
Pulling itself and the sky in dark red
Over the edge of the earth.

—Pattiann Rogers,
"Suppose Your Father
Was a Redbird"

Common loon
have seen about 7-10 so
far — most on Day 1.

I might learn. In this way, I can tell a very complete story of a place—how it looked, what plants were there, any tracks I saw and to whom they belonged. I can know who was hiding from the hawk, who was eating the mesquite beans, what smelled so sweet. I can't do this without entering into a very conscious and focused state of awareness. It is a different sort of journaling than simply writing whatever comes to mind. It is intense and careful work, and not for the faint of heart. I do this using what I call "practiced study," a combination of keeping a daily log, note-taking for the purposes of description and identification, and "thought" exercises. To round it all out, I will sometimes throw in a map for spatial orientation. If all these are done with care, the result is a full, rich picture of place and experience.

Field Notes

GENERAL ORGANIZATION

In the world of taxonomic classification, people who prefer to lump closely related subspecies into one species are called, well, "lumpers;" their counterparts, who would prefer to make the subspecies separate species, are called "splitters." I suspect that most people fall into similar categories in their preferences for the overall organization of their journals. That is, there are those who prefer to keep one notebook and lump everything in it, and there are those who go to the other extreme and keep a separate notebook for everything. I fall somewhere in between. I keep one general notebook when I am on my home ground and others that are just for specific field work. My lumper journal tends to be filled with random, seemingly unrelated items. One day I might be keeping a record of what wildflowers were blooming on a running trail, and another I might be jotting notes to myself for an essay I'm writing. The only consistent things about the entries are that they are all written in my hometown, and they are more or less in chronological order. Sometimes I put a date on the page, sometimes I don't. Sometimes I make note of my exact location, sometimes I don't. It all depends on what was needed for the entry.

My field excursion notebooks, however, are a different story. I usually keep only one per location—I have a notebook for each of my trips down the Missouri River in Montana, one for a trip to the Boundary Waters, and so on. Each day, I start a new journal entry with daily log notes, and these are followed by species of birds and plants I've seen, descriptive landscape notes, and commentary on the journey itself. They are definitely more organized than my lumper notebooks, but it is still a loose organization.

When I was a practicing geologist, however, my notebooks were especially organized. I wanted to be sure that not only could I go back in a few years' time and recreate the data I collected in the field but that someone following in my footsteps could do so from my notebooks as well. As a consequence, there was a very specific format that I used, and it looked something like the journal entries on pages 122 and 123.

Page 123 shows the start of a new day, with a log of location, date, time, and weather. The "stops" correspond with locations I have noted on a separate topographic map; they in turn have accompanying notes on rock samples I've collected at those stops, along with the outlined sample numbered. Page 122 shows a short, narrative summary of the previous day's events (which in this instance included a blown-out tire). It is fairly precise and no-nonsense. Any sketching I did usually involved the order of bedding planes or their orientation (along with compass readings). This is not to say that there wasn't the occasional camp recipe thrown into the notebooks or a short commentary on where to find a place for a clean shower. But the notebooks had a specific purpose, and for the most part I stuck to that.

My point is that the organization of your naturalist's notebook will depend in large part on what your purpose is in keeping it. These days, my informational needs run more to the literary than the scientific, and my notebooks have evolved accordingly. Some of you may find that it suits you to be lumpers, while others may desire or need the precision of splitting the information into highly organized categories. Whatever format you decide to use, here are some questions you might address at the start:

1. **One notebook or many?**
   Some people, as I said on the previous page, keep separate notebooks for everything, while others put it all into one big tome. Lumper or splitter? You decide.

2. **Are your notebooks determined by time or place?**
   Notebooks can be organized according to the years in which they are written or the places they describe.

Descriptive text can be just as important as sketches when documenting your experience in the field.

Summary – Stop 41 was one I did not attend. Had a blowout on the way and Cal and Melanie didn't notice I wasn't behind them, and so went on w/o me. Until then, everything was serpentine. They report that it end in a possible slide of Hayfork. That is to say, the rx were positively identified as Hayfork whether it was a slide is in question.

Tomorrow we are going to drive down Sucker Creek road looking at rx on the way to Cave Junction, where we will buy a new tire.

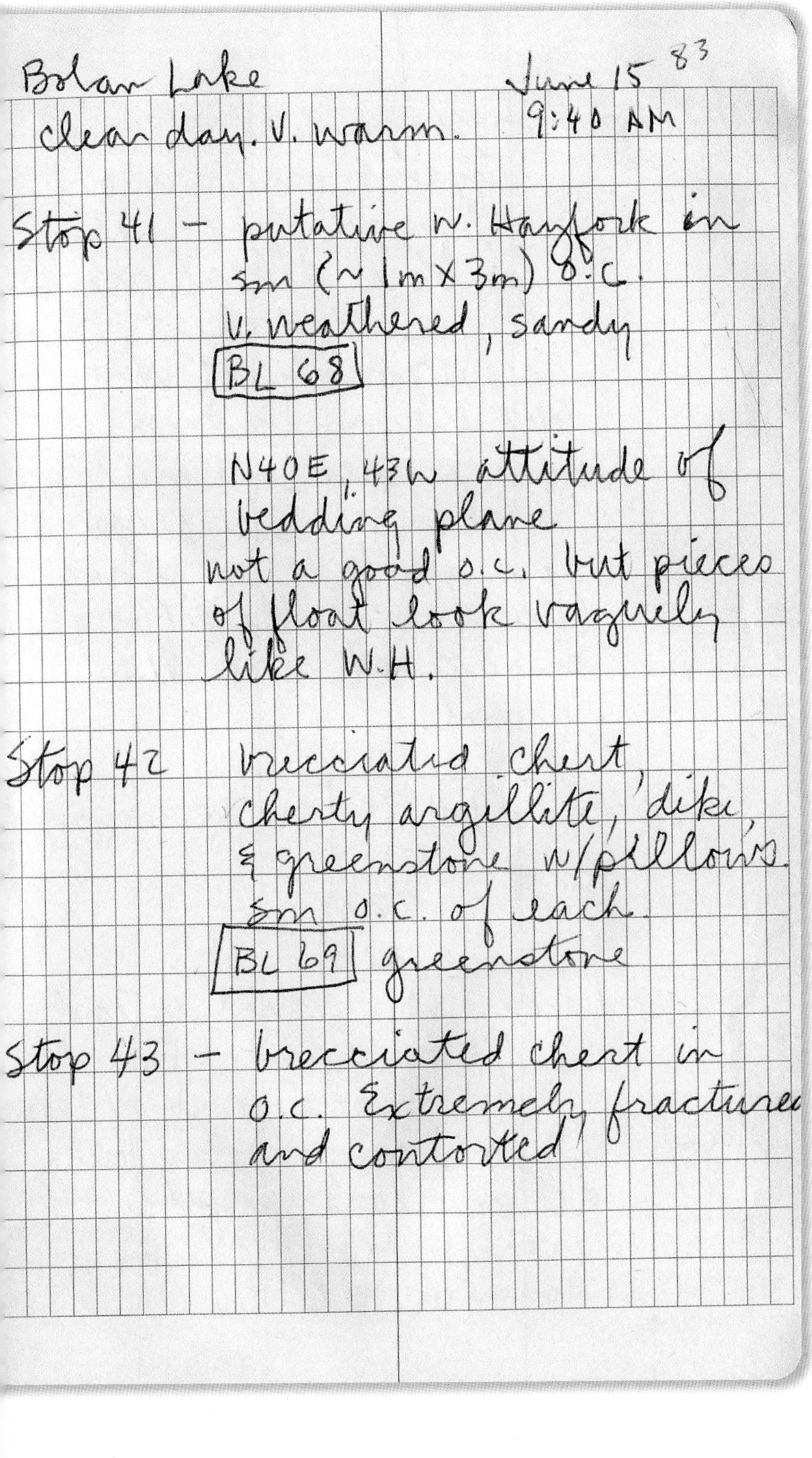

Bolan Lake   June 15 83
clean day. v. warm.   9:40 AM

Stop 41 — putative w. Hayfork in
          sm (~ 1m x 3m) o.c.
          v. weathered, sandy
          BL 68

          N40E, 43W attitude of
          bedding plane
          not a good o.c. but pieces
          of float look vaguely
          like W.H.

Stop 42   brecciated chert,
          cherty argillite, dike,
          & greenstone w/pillows.
          sm o.c. of each.
          BL 69 greenstone

Stop 43 — brecciated chert in
          o.c. Extremely fractured
          and contorted

3. **Front and back, or front only?**
   Some people prefer to write on only one side of a page, leaving the other open for future, additional entries. Others, like me, are cheap and prefer not to waste what amounts to half the notebook.

4. **New page or continuous entries?**
   Do you want to start each new entry on a new page, or do you want to start the new entry right below the previous one?

5. **Numbers or no?**
   Do you want to number your pages? It isn't a bad idea—but you might wait until the journal is complete. Many a time I've torn a page from a journal to use for something unrelated to the field notebook. If I had numbered them ahead of time, I might find myself wondering what was on that missing page.

Over time you'll probably find, as I have, that your preferences for organization will evolve into a format that is comfortable and usable for your needs. I believe that *how* you organize something is less important than having a recognizable, easily followed, consistent format (especially in the case of data collection!). Now we can go on to *what* to put in your journal.

THE DAILY LOG

A ship's deck log is a running record that records the ordinary—as well as the occasional extraordinary—events, every day of the year, for as long as the ship is in commission. Deck logs are not narratives. They aren't places for recording information in story form; rather, this is where the captain makes a list of events and their chronology over a twenty-four-hour period. The type of information included in a log is variable, ranging from the location of the ship at sea and prisoners taken in battle, to accidents, illnesses, deaths, passengers on board, meteorological events, and so on. Because it is in list form, it is very easy and efficient to keep. This is not to say, however, that a story can't be derived from the cumulative information included in a log. On the contrary, deck logs are valuable resources because they allow us to a look at the ordinary—for it is the ordinary, the everyday, that gives us the truest picture of life.

I like to use something like a ship's deck log as a means of keeping long-term records about everyday happenings, such as the things that go on in my backyard or on my walk to work. I also have a special place—a trail through a restored prairie—I run often enough that I can keep track of seasonal changes in this way. I also find that notes like these help me pick up on different patterns. For example, cold fronts follow certain cloud patterns and wind directions. If I am keeping a daily log of these two things, I will see this reflected in my notebooks.

These notes don't have to be especially complex, just consistent. In addition to the date and time of day, I'll record the weather, any birds I happen to see, what is in flower, and so on. Consistent notes taken over a long period of time can be invaluable in tracking changes in ecosystems.

In fact, this kind of routine data collection, done over the course of years, is something that has potential value to science. For a variety of reasons, many scientists don't have the luxury of doing studies in which data are collected over a period of several years. Yet long-term data are some of the most useful we have for understanding ecological and environmental trends. But this is not to say that long-term data are never collected. Some scientists do it as a matter of course in the same sort of everyday record-keeping that we are talking about here. When global warming was first seriously proposed as a hypothesis, one of the criticisms leveled against it was a lack of long-term data to support it. Such data, taken as everyday meteorological readings and population counts for a period of years, now exist. As a result, today nearly all scientists accept the disturbing change in climate and its effects as scientific fact.

But scientists are not the only source of information about changes in global climate. Gardeners long have had a tradition of careful journaling. For well over a hundred years, there has been a steady gathering of dates when the first irises bloomed, when the bees returned, or how many inches of rain fell. In particular, scientists are now finding that these journals—each originally kept for no other reason than the owner's desire to make notes about the garden—are providing valuable clues to long-term changes in our ecosystem and further contributing to their understanding about global warming. A few years ago, a news story on National Public Radio reported that retired schoolteacher Mary Manning had kept notes on her daffodils since 1965. That was the year she first became curious about a comment her mother had made some years before about her daffodils blooming by Easter. Mary Manning realized that the daffodils she'd planted were in fact blooming much earlier in the season and decided, out of plain old curiosity, to start keeping a record of the blooming dates of the flowers in her garden. As the reporter of the piece, Daniel Grossman, notes, 1965 was long before scientists began to suspect that something was changing in our global climate. Great Britain has long been home to many ardent gardeners and nature observers, and the journals that they've been keeping are starting to provide clues to professional ecologists about climate changes. In fact, one such ecologist, Alistair Fitter, used his own father's journals to determine that the blooming dates of some species of plants have shifted, on average, two weeks every ten years. This is a remarkable change in a relatively short period of time. The important point I'd like to make here is that global weather changes might have gone unnoticed without the careful efforts of individuals making notes in a journal.

Making consistent, careful notes about nature takes information out of the realm of anecdotal evidence (i.e., I remember back when daffodils bloomed later in the season) and puts it squarely in the realm of data (daffodils bloomed on this date back in 1978).

The field of ornithology is another area where serious amateurs are regularly recruited for their abilities to take the time to count birds. This has been the case for the annual Audubon Christmas Count in which over a century of recorded data have been used to track the general abundance and diversity of bird populations. The more recently initiated Breeding Bird Survey, conducted by the United States Geological Survey, enlists the aid of numerous volunteers each spring and summer to record data across the continental United States.

In addition to these examples in which all the species of North American birds are studied as part of the data, careful longitudinal record-keeping or "ordinary" data can contribute to the understanding of a single species. Perhaps the most well-known instance of an amateur naturalist contributing to our knowledge of a species is the case of Margaret Morse Nice, who studied the song sparrows in her Ohio backyard for eight years. The result was a two-volume study covering virtually every aspect of that bird's life history. Although not formally trained as an ornithologist, Nice was internationally recognized for her contributions to ornithology. She became a Fellow of the American Ornithologists' Union (AOU) and the first woman president of the Wilson Ornithological Society (then the Wilson Club). The AOU has since established a fund in her name, and the Wilson Society has named a medal in her honor.

All this serves to underscore the value in routine record-keeping. Like the ship's log mentioned at the start of this section, it is the collected body of everyday notation that ultimately gives us the richest picture of life lived. The same is true about our interactions with nature. So when you go out into the field, concentrate on the little things as well as the big. Record all of them that you can. Become part of a long tradition.

Starting Your Daily Log

To get started recording your own "ship's log," you might use the following checklist at first and see how it works for you. Later, you may decide that you want to include additional routine observations and leave some others out. Ultimately you will be creating your vision of the natural world in your notebooks. In any case, select the data you want to record every time you go out to the field and do your best to stick to it. In time, these simple records provide a living history of a place.

In all of these entries, keep in mind that you always want to include enough clear information that you could return to the journal years hence and know exactly where you were, what the date was, what you saw, and so on. This is especially important if you anticipate that someone else will need to use your notes for future work. Here are things I log at the top of the page each time I start out with the intent to record my day in the field:

- Location
     specific location, city, county, state
- Date
     10 June 2008 or June 10, 2008 is more likely to be universally understood than is 6/10/08
- Time of day
- Weather
     sky (Are there clouds? If so, what kind?)
     wind speed and direction (don't forget your Beaufort scale)
     moisture (humidity, rainfall, etc.)
     temperature

I also start a running log of anything I might see over the course of my outing. These might include the following:

- birds
- flowers in bloom
- animal tracks and sign
- habitat

A sample entry for my daily log might look something like this:

LLL ~10:20a June 18
T ~78° W ~12-15
partly cloudy

Things heard and seen on
run along Long Trail:

Bob White
Bullock's Oriole
RT hawk (being mobbed
by GT Grackle)
E Meadowlark
Cassin's Sp
CottonTail
Yellow bladderpod
Tahoka daisy
Sunflower
purple Thistle
wasps (3 where I sit
writing this)
Broom weed?
W. Kingbird

You'll notice I have used a simple code for *time of day* (a = A.M., p = P.M.), *temperature* (T), *wind* (W), and *place* (LLL = Lubbock Lake Landmark). I also have standard abbreviations that I use for birds I commonly find along the trail: Cassin's sp. = Cassin's sparrow, RT hawk = red-tailed hawk, and so on. As you can see, this sort of entry is nothing fancy and can be jotted down in a matter of a few minutes of observation. It's a good habit to get into for all the reasons I've mentioned.

A word about the use of abbreviations, however: use them sparingly and only when they are either obvious or you have explained them clearly somewhere in the journal. Remember, the aim is to be able to look back in the journal in a few years and understand what you were observing at the time.

NOTE-TAKING FOR STUDY AND IDENTIFICATION

Notes we take in order to gather information for identification or further study on a subject of interest are different from our daily log or descriptive entries. Whereas the daily log is something that can, with practice, be jotted down in a very brief space of time, note-taking for the purpose of information requires that we gather as much detail as possible. Often, especially when we are looking at something entirely new to us, we don't know what piece of information will turn out to be valuable.

Mastering the fine art of detailed record-keeping, such as the number of petals and stamens a flower has or whether that bird you saw had a broken eye ring, will help you in the task of identification. For example, identifying between some species of birds can depend on field marks so subtle that even experts are sometimes stumped. To illustrate this, let's say you're in the field describing a flycatcher you've seen, and you happen to note that it has a *pale* yellow breast and some rufous (what birders call a rusty shade of red) under its tail. Later, once you're snug back in your study, you can check your field guide and be certain that it was the ash-throated flycatcher and not a wayward great-crested flycatcher. My point is this: it might be relatively easy to figure out that you've seen a flycatcher, and the rufous tail, plus range maps, will help you to narrow it down to these two birds, but it is the pale yellow breast that tells you what you saw. *If you didn't happen to make a note of that key field mark, you would not be able to identify the bird with certainty when you later looked it up in the guide.*

This is also a good time to use the techniques you've learned for drawing for identification. Although there may be times to draw for artistic effect, here our aim is simple, straightforward information with plenty of detail.

Page 131 shows another sample page from Robert Waller's notebook. This exercise involved first drawing and making notes for information using a known subject (in this case, a yucca plant), followed by drawing an unknown subject. By drawing a known plant first and thinking about what it is that makes that plant distinct as a species (as opposed to some other species), you can develop a sense of what kind of information is useful in identifying a different plant.

Note the sort of information that Robert chose to include in his portrait of both the yucca and the plant he later identified as a prairie coneflower: overall size, size of the seedpods or heads, shape of seeds and leaves, colors, and so on. He also chose to do an overall drawing of the plantas well as a detailed drawing of the seed heads. Other things he might have included, but didn't, are the shapes and sizes of the seeds themselves. Still, this is a very good journal entry— good enough to enable him to compare his notes and drawings against a field guide and come up with the plant identification.

There are other types of information you can include in your field notes. Pages 132 and 133 show a journal entry by Delilah Clark, where she not only included plants but also birds and bird behavior, animal holes and their natural history, and a map of her location. Rather than being a focused look at a specific animal or plant, this is an overall portrait of a place that she visited one day to take some landscape photos. The field notebook, in this instance, provides some excellent background information for one of her other interests, photography.

As you can see, Delilah made use of frames to provide some order to her information. Her frames are not very complicated, just simple lines to form boxes. No matter—they do the job nicely. (Note also Delilah's daily log in the top left-hand corner.)

You can also do follow-up field notes to further enhance your learning. Pages 134 and 135 show a wonderful example from Mary Porter's journal, where she explains some research on red-winged blackbirds, noting behavior patterns she'd seen in the field. In it, she references a book by Les Beletsky about red-winged blackbirds.

Drawing for Information

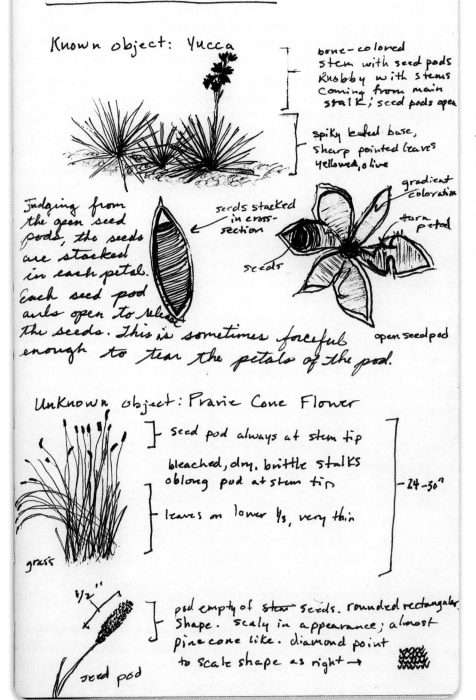

Known object: Yucca

bone-colored
stem with seed pods
Knobby with stems
coming from main
stalk; seed pods open

spiky leafed base,
sharp pointed leaves
yellowed, olive

gradient
coloration

torn
petal

seeds

open seedpod

Judging from
the open seed
pods, the seeds
are stacked
in each petal.
Each seed pod
curls open to release
the seeds. This is sometimes forceful
enough to tear the petals of the pod.

seeds stacked
in cross-
section

Unknown object: Prarie Cone Flower

grass

Seed pod always at stem tip

bleached, dry, brittle stalks
oblong pod at stem tip

leaves on lower 1/3, very thin

24-30"

1/2"

seed pod

pod empty of star seeds. rounded rectangular.
Shape. scaly in appearance; almost
pinecone like. diamond point
to scale shape as right →

Robert Waller's journal shows how observation of a known object can be used to identify key features of an unknown object.

Delilah Clark used a variety of elements to create an overall portrait of a place she visited.

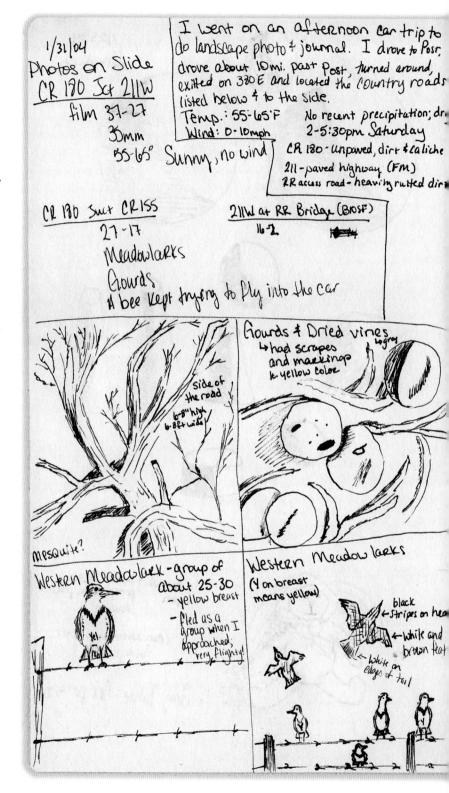

1/31/04
Photos on Slide
CR 180 Jct 211W
film 37-27
35mm
55-65°

I went on an afternoon car trip to do landscape photo & journal. I drove to Post, drove about 10mi. past Post, turned around, exitted on 380 E and located the country roads listed below & to the side.
Temp.: 55-65°F   No recent precipitation; dr
Wind: 0-10mph   2-5:30pm Saturday
Sunny, no wind   CR 180 - unpaved, dirt & caliche
211 - paved highway (FM)
2R access road - heavily rutted dir

CR 180 Jnct CR 155
27-17
Meadowlarks
Gourds
A bee kept trying to fly into the car

211W at RR Bridge (BNSF)
16-2

Mesquite?
Western Meadowlark - group of about 25-30
- yellow breast
- Yel.
- fled as a group when I approached; very flighty!

Gourds & Dried vines
↳ had scrapes and markings
to gray
k- yellow color

Western Meadow larks
(Y on breast means yellow)
black
←stripes on hea
←white and brown feat
←white on edges of tail

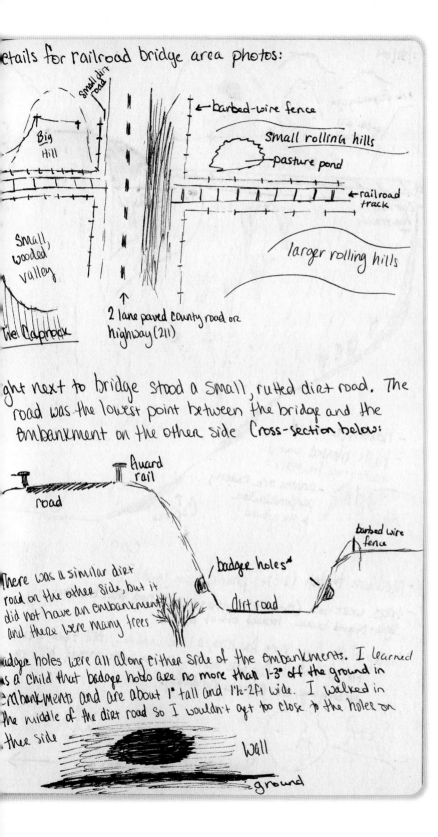

etails for railroad bridge area photos:

small dirt road

Big Hill

barbed-wire fence

small rolling hills

pasture pond

railroad track

Small, wooded valley

larger rolling hills

The Caprock

2 lane paved county road or highway (211)

ght next to bridge stood a small, rutted dirt road. The road was the lowest point between the bridge and the embankment on the other side Cross-section below:

Guard rail

road

barbed wire fence

There was a similar dirt road on the other side, but it did not have an embankment and there were many trees

badger holes

dirt road

adger holes were all along either side of the embankments. I learned s a child that badger holes are no more than 1-3° off the ground in embankments and are about 1° tall and 1½-2ft wide. I walked in the middle of the dirt road so I wouldn't get too close to the holes on their side

Wall

ground

Research on the Red-Winged Blackbird:

Funny story on their vocalizations — When a song is played through a loadspeaker of a male Red-winged blackbird in another males territory, the experimen[t] male will approach the speak[er] + behave aggressivly toward i[t] treating it like anothe male Red-winged Blackbird that must be evicted from his territory.

The Song

Males can recognize each other as individuals not only by their appeerence, but by the sound of their call.

In male-male threat, singing is used for territorial maintenance + defense as a signaling threat.
• males w/territories sing more often than tho[se] "floaters" w/out

Mary Porter compared her own observations with an expert resource to confirm her research on the red-winged blackbird.

"Sometimes the male flies 1st into the vegetation + is followed by an interested female. The male puts his wings out + up, forming a V above his back, aims his bill down into the vegetation, + 'growls'." (p124)

⇩

This sounds very similar to what I was seeing a male do at Buffalo Springs Lake. However, I could not see any females involved, just two other males. It is suggested that this is a nest sight demonstration. But researchers have never found nest in areas where they saw this display occur. So I don't think that was what my male was doing.

— ✳ — ✳ — ✳ — ✳ — ✳ — ✳ — ✳

"Territories that interface w/ the open water of a lake have very high [insect] emergence rates." (p155)

Territory

⇩

This could explain why all three males were making call from cat tail perches close to the water's edge. So maybe their calls + displays were in an effort to secure a resourceful territory.

⟵ fabulous

EXERCISES

1. Try this exercise to learn how to pick out key field marks. First, find something that you can already identify, such as a flower, bird, or even your cat or dog. Do a detailed "drawing for identification" of it. Make notes of those features that make it uniquely "that" thing and not something else. One way to figure out what features to use is to ask yourself, "Why is this an iris and not a daisy?" or "What makes this dog a miniature schnauzer and not a Great Dane or Chihuahua?"
2. Now find something that you don't already know. Do the same sort of drawing and include those things that will help you identify it on the *macro* scale (i.e., is it a grass or is it a flower?), as well as on the *micro* scale (that is, what species of grass is it?). The macro scale is usually pretty obvious (for example, gull versus sparrow); it is the micro scale on which we really need to concentrate to get the most useful information (what species of gull?). One way to figure out what the useful micro features might be is to look around and see if there are any other different species of the same thing in the area. If there are, try to determine what makes your unknown different from the other species of the same thing. Draw the unknown subject and make note of what you think might be the key field marks.

   Once you get to a place where you can look up the subject in a field guide, see if you can identify it. If you can, pat yourself on the back and ink the name of the subject beside its picture.

   If you can't identify it, try to figure out what key information you are missing. This will help you get better at drawing and note-taking for study and identification in the future.

DESCRIPTIVE NOTES

Once I have my daily log underway, I often take just a few moments to heighten my awareness by paying attention to each of my senses. Again, this doesn't have to be anything complicated; its purpose is simply to make me slow down and start paying attention to my surroundings. Some examples of these notes are as follows:

- leaves or grass rustling
- birds singing or calling
- wind on my skin
- sun warming my hair
- smell of rain in the air

When making these sorts of observations, I like to warm up my descriptive muscles by trying to find the freshest, least clichéd, most perfect words for the sensation I'm recording. A simple exercise that I sometimes use for this is a variation on a wonderful technique described by Natalie Goldberg in *Writing Down the Bones*. I think first about the subject whose action I want to describe—let's say it's the wind blowing through the grass in this case. Then I think about another subject that is completely unrelated. It helps if the second subject has lots of action verbs associated with it (Goldberg uses the occupation of "cook" in the example in her book), so I might pick "carpenter" for mine. Then I think of action verbs associated with woodworking and plug them into sentences about the wind in my head:

> "The wind *sawed* through the grass."
> "The wind *hammered* at the grass."

And so on. Sometimes it works especially well; sometimes I can't find any combination of action verbs that I like. In this case, I don't think either is working. When this happens, I pick a different action verb/subject and try again. Or sometimes one of the action verbs I've used might trigger others that are unrelated to woodworking, so *sawed* becomes *chopped*, which becomes *chipped, slapped, zipped, snicked, sizzled, buzzed, popped,* and so on.

Here is a sentence about the sensory effect of wind blowing through the grass that I came up with using this thought process. I pick it out of the lineup simply because I think the pairing of words is interesting:

> "The grass *sizzles* in the wind."

This, for some reason, has the effect of making me think of bees (not surprising, since I am generally obsessed with them—but that's another story), which I turn into something more homespun (and more my "voice"):

> "The grass stirs, like it's full of bees."

The point is not to come up with combinations that are so odd as to be jarring but to find a fresh way of describing things with words that are *just right*. In this example, I like the idea of grass moving around in the wind as if it's being stirred up by bees—it's more interesting to me to think about than the more commonly used "rustling" or "whispering" to describe this sensory effect.[1] And for that matter, if we're going to talk about grass as if it were capable of

---

1. I liked this so much, in fact, that after coming up with it in this exercise, I wrote an essay and used "bees in the grass" to describe the sound of the wind where I live.

having conversation, then grass that's full of bees probably has much more on its mind, don't you think?

Again, this is a warm-up exercise to help keep my notes fresh and interesting. I may not use the sentence at all to describe what is going on, but it serves to wake me up to possibilities. It has the effect of concentrating my mind on the task at hand, which is recording my experience in the field. If I can clear my head of clichés, I am much more open to what is really happening around me. On the other hand, it doesn't pay to sit around and contemplate the "perfect" action verb for an hour, either. Sometimes a plain and simple *sit, run, walk, wave* is just what is needed, but if I come to that conclusion, it is because I've made that choice of words and not because I was asleep and snoring in the middle of a sentence.

EXERCISES

1. What kind of information do you think might be useful to collect over a long period of time? What would you want to know about a day if you were to look back on it weeks, months, or even years later and you wanted to recreate it? Create a daily log, then make a template and paste it on the inside cover of your journal to use as a reference. *Hint: Leave blank spaces on the list so that as you use it over several outings, you can refine it by adding or subtracting categories.* Also, be sure to include the key to any codes for shorthand that you develop. If you are just starting out, of course, you may not yet know the names of many birds and plants, but if you leave some blank spaces on the code list, you can add to this as you go along. By the time you're ready to move on to another journal, you'll have a daily log checklist that reflects your personal interests. At that point, you probably will not need a template or code list to assist your memory, but if you do, you can always make a master list to photocopy for pasting in later journals.

2. Go to the place where you'd like to make your first journal entry (it could be a trail, park, or even your backyard) and jot down your daily log. Then take a few moments to try the descriptor exercise outlined on the previous page. Pick one or two sensory characteristics (smell, sound, etc.) and try to find a fresh and *perfect* descriptor for it.

3. We've seen how useful the Beaufort scale can be for determining wind speed. Can you come up with similar "scales" for knowing time of day without a watch? Compass direction without a compass? Temperature without a thermometer? If you can, make a copy of these and paste them in your notebook for reference.

4. Try Natalie Goldberg's "pairings" exercise. Find two or three commonplace things to describe while out in the field and make them fresh. Pick seemingly unrelated subjects, assign action verbs to them, and let the mind begin its work.

THOUGHT EXERCISES

Finally, as a means of observing the natural history of a place with fresh eyes, I often find it useful to practice assigning myself writing and sketching exercises of my own devising. For example, if I happen upon coyote scat, I might stop and make a quick drawing of it. Some of the things I might notice as I'm doing so would be that one end of each piece of scat is pointed (this is not the case with all organisms and is therefore a useful field mark for this species). I might also notice the pointed ends all seem to be oriented in the same direction. These two observations lead me to form the following questions: Which end—the pointed or rounded end—hits the ground first (i.e., which comes out of the coyote's butt first)? Can I tell from this observation which way he was facing when he squatted? If so, what was he looking at when he relieved himself? (At this point I might put myself on the coyote's eye level and try to figure that out.)

Then I might look at the scat itself. How fresh is it? Can I tell what he's been eating? If I can't tell, I might ask myself, "What sort of prey/plants live around here for him to eat? Who is afraid of Mr. Coyote?" I know kangaroo mice live in the area, because I've seen their holes and tracks . . . and this area is chock-full of prairie dogs . . .

Who should Mr. Coyote fear? Are there predators living here large enough to threaten him, or am I the only thing the coyote needs to worry about?

If I continue along the trail, I might also find other piles of scat lying in the middle of the path. (This is, in fact, something I've noticed quite a bit.) Is it the same coyote? A different one? Why are the piles always in the middle of the path? Is he marking territory, or does he feel safest doing his business here, where he can see any threats coming during what is arguably a vulnerable moment? Finally, I might ask myself where all these phantom coyotes are hiding out. Can I see likely places to look for dens?

By this time, I've spent quite a few minutes forming a natural history portrait from simply looking at a pile of scat lying in the middle of a path. The scat itself might be interesting, but what makes it really intriguing are the clues it holds to a story. I could have walked right past it—made a quick mental note of its presence (or not even that) and moved on. Instead, I tried to use it as a springboard for questions, most of which I won't have immediate answers for. If I am lucky or clever, however, I might be able to figure some of them out, and the others I could probably look up once I got back to my library. In this way, I've learned a great deal about

EXERCISES

1. Pick a quiet place somewhere outside and sit down. First, note the weather (temperature, sky, wind), time of day, and location. Next, sketch a brief map of the place where you are sitting, labeling the important parts. Next, using one-word names or descriptors, make a comprehensive inventory of any birds, animals, and plants you can identify (if there is more than one individual for a particular species, be sure to note the number. Five red-winged blackbirds, for example). Next, if there are animals or birds, note the behavior. Take a few minutes to make a couple of sketches of things that look interesting to you.

2. Pick one of the things on your list and think of one question about it that you would like to know. For example, you might ask, "What do red-winged blackbirds eat?" Try to answer this question using your powers of observation.

3. Try to imagine the last twenty-four hours in the life of your subject. Using a simple list, make note of events that might have occurred during this period. Make an effort to really think about this from the perspective of your subject. Take a cue from Pattiann Rogers and try to imagine what dawn looks like to a red-winged blackbird. What is it like when night falls? If you come up with questions you cannot readily answer from actual observations, make a note of these questions in the margins. For example: Where do red-winged blackbirds sleep? You can make a guess, but note it as such.

4. Write a poem of "supposition" about something you observe.

coyotes without ever having seen one that day. And even more than that, I've caught a glimpse into the community through which I am traveling.

This is one example of a thought exercise, but there are many other possibilities. You could let your imagination roam and try to figure out the paths the coyote takes during the day—maybe even make a "thought map" of its day. Or you could try to picture what a red-tailed hawk sees when it flies. What does the wind sound like to it?

The possibilities for thought exercises like these are endless, and they make a very good vehicle for training ourselves to notice what is going on around us. I think that the poem from which I drew the epigram for this chapter is a wonderful example of a thought exercise. In it, Pattiann Rogers challenges you to imagine yourself as a young cardinal and reflect on how it would shape your vision of the world if, as she says in an explanation of the poem, "everything good you knew in the world came from a redbird."[2] The poem in its entirety is shown on the following page.

2. Pattiann Rogers, *The Dream of the Marsh Wren,* Milkweed Editions, 1999.

Suppose Your Father Was a Redbird

Pattiann Rogers

Suppose his body was the meticulous
    layering
Of graduated down which you studied early,
Rows of feather increasing in size to the
    hard-splayed
Wine-gloss tips of his outer edges.

Suppose, before you could speak, you
    watched
The slow spread of his wing over and over,
The appearance of that invisible appendage,
The unfolding transformation of his body to
    the airborne.
And you followed his departure again and
    again,
Learning to distinguish the red microbe of
    his being
Far into the line of the horizon.

Then today you might be the only one able
    to see
The breast of a single red bloom
Five miles away across an open field.
The modification of your eye might have
    enabled you
To spot a red moth hanging on an oak
    branch
In the exact center of the Aurorean Forest.
And you could define for us "hearing red in
    the air,"

As you predict the day pollen from the
    poppy
Will blow in from the valley.

Naturally you would picture your faith
    arranged
In filamented principles moving from pink
To crimson at the final quill. And the red
    tremble
Of your dream you might explain as the
    shimmer
Of his back lost over the sea at dawn.
Your sudden visions you might interpret as
    the uncreasing
Of heaven, the bones of the sky spread,
The conceptualized wing of the mind
    untangling.

Imagine the intensity of your revelation
The night the entire body of a star turns red
And you watch it as it rushes in flames
Across the black, down into the hills.

If your father was a redbird,
Then you would be obligated to try to
    understand
What it is you recognized in the sun
As you study it again this evening
Pulling itself and the sky in dark red
Over the edge of the earth.

Pattiann Rogers was inspired to write the poem after the successful rescue and return of a baby cardinal to its very protective father. She describes the drama in her book, *The Dream of the Marsh Wren*, and calls this a poem of "supposition." Try to come up with some thought exercises for yourself—perhaps you should even try to write your own poem of supposition about the subject of your exercise. It may feel awkward and frustrating at first, but it will get easier if you keep at it.

Maps

When we think of maps, what usually comes to mind are those maps and bulky road atlases we use to navigate the nation's highway system. While it is true that these are an indispensable part of our lives, it is limiting to assume that a set of driving directions is all that a map can be. Maps can and should read as a text or narrative—a visual representation of information. Moreover, maps are an insight into what the mapmaker thinks is important. By choosing what to include or leave off a map, the mapmaker decides what knowledge of a place should be recorded for the rest of the world to see. Maps, in fact, can even sometimes tell us something about a mapmaker's beliefs and values, something that can be both a positive and negative thing. Finally, maps can be visually beautiful, whether they are whimsical or strictly utilitarian.

If you stop for a moment and think about it, you could probably come up with a much wider range of maps with which you are familiar: green and brown topographic maps with their fine web of lines, three-dimensional maps with bumpy ridges and mountains, maps in field guides showing the range of a particular species, and long, narrow maps that help you know where you are on a twisting, winding river.

Perhaps it is this last piece of knowledge—where we are—that we most associate with maps. Indeed, I think that for the naturalist in the field, this is one of the best reasons to include maps in your journal entries. You are saying, in effect, "I am here at this moment in time. This is what I am experiencing. This is what is important to me. This is what I value."

It isn't necessary to include maps in your journal, but it provides another expression for ideas and information. The maps can be as simple or complex as you wish to make them. On the following pages are examples of maps that were used to enhance the documentation of a particular field experience.

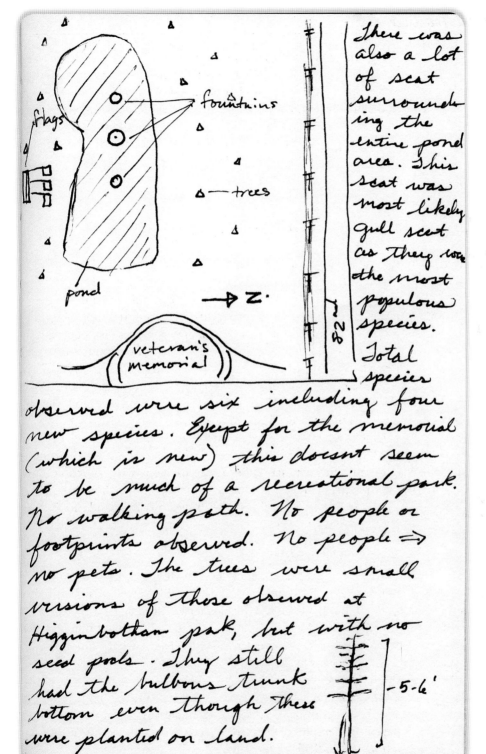

There was also a lot of scat surrounding the entire pond area. This scat was most likely gull scat as they were the most populous species. Total species observed were six including four new species. Except for the memorial (which is new) this doesn't seem to be much of a recreational park. No walking path. No people or footprints observed. No people ⇒ no pets. The trees were small versions of those observed at Higginbotham park, but with no seed pods. They still had the bulbous trunk bottom even though these were planted on land.

A map by Robert Waller, to accompany text in his journal. You can see that the map need not be complicated to add to the text.

A rather whimsical map by Mary Porter showing a campsite on the Texas Colorado River. It is apparent that the "poo box" is among the things Mary found notable on the trip!

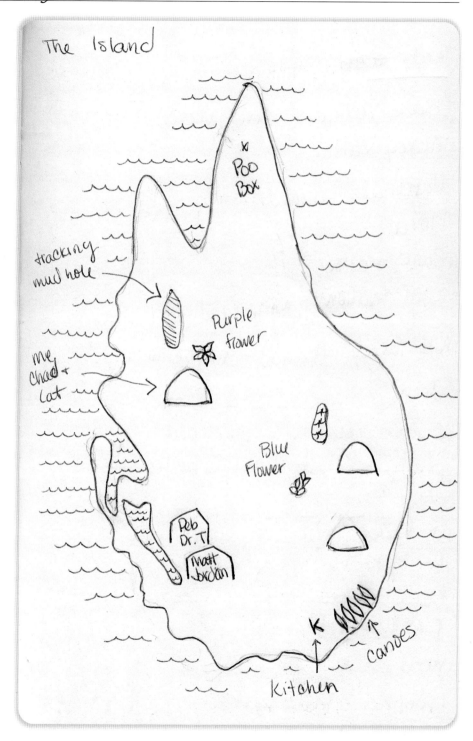

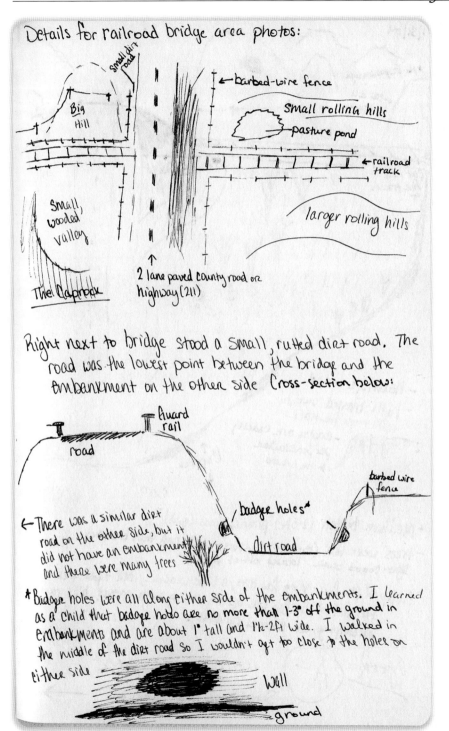

Details for railroad bridge area photos:

small dirt road

Big Hill

barbed-wire fence

Small rolling hills

pasture pond

railroad track

Small, wooded valley

larger rolling hills

The Caprock

2 lane paved county road or highway (211)

Right next to bridge stood a small, rutted dirt road. The road was the lowest point between the bridge and the embankment on the other side. Cross-section below:

Guard rail

road

← There was a similar dirt road on the other side, but it did not have an embankment and there were many trees

barbed wire fence

badger holes*

dirt road

* Badger holes were all along either side of the embankments. I learned as a child that badger holes are no more than 1-3" off the ground in embankments and are about 1" tall and 1½-2ft wide. I walked in the middle of the dirt road so I wouldn't get too close to the holes on either side

Well

ground

A map by Delilah Clark showing a site she used for some of her photographs. She has also included a cross-sectional view below the map for further clarification.

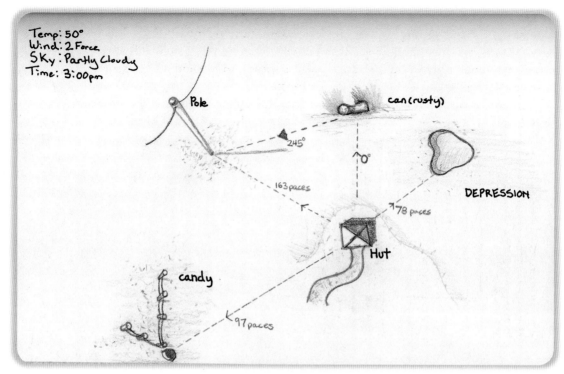

Temp: 50°
Wind: 2 Force
Sky: Partly Cloudy
Time: 3:00pm

Pole

can (rusty)

245°

0°

163 paces

DEPRESSION

78 paces

Hut

candy

97 paces

A map by Jay Daniel, made for an orienteering exercise in the Fieldcraft class (one in which finding a tin of candy was part of the assignment). Note that he has it in three dimensions.

These are maps that largely serve as text. With the exception of Jay's map, they don't represent a set of geographical directions for the purpose of finding something; rather, they note the things the author believes have value in telling the story of the landscape or experience. The possibilities for the map as text are endless and may include the following:

- daily walks
- where you saw a coyote cross a path
- bicycle routes
- your garden
- recycling locations in your hometown
- good places for birding
- where the first snapdragon blooms

The students have also each used different approaches to their mapmaking, from including cross-sectional views to drawing in three dimensions. In each, however, they have been careful to label symbols. Though no one did it in the examples shown, they could have used a map legend to do this, with an explanation of what each of the symbols means. It is also useful to include a north arrow, as Robert did, to orient the viewer. Though not strictly necessary for all journal maps, it is a practice I can't recommend strongly enough, since without it we are left to assume that the top of the page is north (as is standard on many maps, but not all).

As with other notes in the journal, it's important that you can return to the map in future years and understand what it is that you've drawn. Here are a few tips that will help you with that:

- include a north arrow
- include a map legend, with explanations for symbols
- avoid abbreviations

equisetum &
leaves of common
white water lily
BWCA July 10 '05
Mahlberg Lake

Final Words

By now you should be able to see that there is an almost infinite range of possibilities for your naturalist's notebook, both in terms of the type you choose to keep as well as what you actually put in it. Do you have a garden you love and want to chronicle? Are you a compulsive feeder watcher? Is there a special trip that you will be taking? All of these experiences—as well as many others—easily lend themselves to the pleasures of the journal record. Think of the suggestions in this book as a starting point from which you can expand and grow your own vision. If you make the process of keeping the journal pleasant and enjoyable, you will return to it again and again. Over time, your journal will evolve to be a rich, full record of the natural world. More importantly, it will become a reflection of the knowledge you've gained in the process.

Annotated Bibliography

REFERENCES AND WORKS CITED

Beletsky, Les. *The Red-Winged Blackbird: The Biology of a Strongly Polygynous Songbird*. San Diego: Academic Press, 1996.

Brown, Greg. "Two Little Feet." In *Further In*. Leeds, United Kingdom: Red House Music, 1996.

Goldberg, Natalie. *Writing Down the Bones: Freeing the Writer Within*. Expanded edition. Boston: Shambhala Publications, Inc., 2005.

Kirkpatrick, Zoe Merriman. *Wildflowers of the Western Plains*. Austin, Texas: University of Texas Press, 1992.

O'Keefe, Georgia. *Georgia O'Keefe*. New York: Penguin Books, 1977.

Oliver, Mary. "Where Does the Temple Begin, Where Does It End?" In *Why I Wake Early*. Boston: Beacon Press, 2005.

Ommundsen, Peter. "Pronunciation of Biological Latin: Including Taxonomic Names of Plants and Animals." Cape West Publishing. http://www.saltspring.com/capewest/pron.htm (accessed May 22, 2009).

Rogers, Pattiann. *The Dream of the Marsh Wren: Writing as Reciprocal Creation*. Minneapolis: Milkweed Editions, 1999.

———. "Suppose Your Father Was a Redbird." In *Firekeeper: Selected Poems*. Minneapolis: Milkweed Editions, 2005. Reprinted with permission from the author.

Stafford, William. "On Being a Person." In *Even in Quiet Places*. Lewiston, Idaho: Confluence Press, 1996.

Stearn, William T. *Stearn's Dictionary of Plants for Gardeners*. Revised edition. London: Cassell Publishers Limited, 1992.

Wenthe, William. "After Moving to a Place Where I Do Not Know the Names of Plants and Birds." In *Not Till We Are Lost*. Baton Rouge, Louisiana: Louisiana State University Press, 2004. Reprinted with permission from the author.

NATURE JOURNALING

Herman, Steven G. *The Naturalist's Field Journal*. Vermillion, South Dakota: Buteo Books, 1986 (an explanation of the Grinnell system of record-keeping).

Hinchman, Hannah. *A Life in Hand: Creating the Illuminated Journal*. Layton, Utah: Peregrine Smith Books, 1991.

———. *A Trail Through Leaves: The Journal As a Path to Place*. New York: W.W. Norton & Company, 1997.

Leslie, Clare Walker, and Charles E. Roth. *Keeping a Nature Journal: Discover a Whole New Way of Seeing the World Around You*. Pownal, Vermont: Storey Publishing, 2000.

FIELD GUIDES AND NATURALIST TECHNIQUES

Dunn, Jon L., and Jonathan Alderfer. *National Geographic Field Guide to the Birds of North America*. 5th ed. Washington, D.C.: National Geographic Society, 1983.

Halfpenny, James C. *Scats and Tracks of the Desert Southwest*. Helena, Montana: Falcon Publishing, 2000 (my favorite field guide).

Merlin, Pinau. *A Field Guide to Desert Holes*. Tucson, Arizona: Arizona-Sonora Desert Museum, 1999.

Rhinehart, Kurt. *Naturalist's Guide to Observing Nature*. Mechanicsburg, Pennsylvania: Stackpole Books, 2006.

Sibley, David Allen. *The Sibley Guide to Birds*. New York: Knopf, 2000.

Stokes, Donald, and Lillian Stokes. *Stokes Guide to Animal Tracking and Behavior*. New York: Little, Brown and Company, 1986.

SKETCHING AND DRAWING

Busby, John. *Drawing Birds*. Portland, Oregon: Timber Press, 2005 (one of the best books on drawing birds).

Leslie, Clare Walker. *The Art of Field Sketching*. Revised printing, Dubuque, Iowa: Kendall Hunt Publishing, 1995 (an excellent book on the subject of field sketching).

Martin, Rosie, and Meriel Thurstan. *Botanical Illustration Course: With the Eden Project*. London: Batsford, 2006 (my personal favorite for botanical illustration techniques).

Nice, Claudia. *How to Keep a Sketchbook Journal*. 1st ed. Cincinnati, Ohio: North Light Books, 2001 (good art instruction).

West, Keith. *How to Draw Plants: The Techniques of Botanical Illustration*. Portland, Oregon: Timber Press, 1996.

Wunderlich, Eleanor B. *Botanical Illustration in Watercolor*. Paperback edition. New York: Watson-Guptill, 1996.

MAPS AND MAPMAKING

Boga, Steven. *Orienteering: The Sport of Navigating with Map and Compass.* Mechanicsburg, Pennsylvania: Stackpole Books, 1997.

Harmon, Katherine. *You Are Here: Personal Geographies and Other Maps of the Imagination.* New York: Princeton Architectural Press, 2004 (not so much about mapmaking as it is about expanding your concept of what a map is—truly a remarkable book).

Hjellström, Björn. *Be Expert with Map and Compass: The Complete Orienteering Handbook.* 5th ed. New York: Hungry Minds, 1994.